CRYSTAL SKULLS

CRYSTAL SKULLS

Emissaries of Healing and Sacred Wisdom

MARION WEBB-DE SISTO

Copyright © 2002 by Marion Webb-De Sisto.

Library of Congress Number: 2002093717
ISBN: Hardcover   1-4010-6994-0
               Softcover   1-4010-6993-2

All rights reserved. No part of this book may be reproduced or transmitted in any form or by any means, electronic or mechanical, including photocopying, recording, or by any information storage and retrieval system, without permission in writing from the copyright owner.

This book was printed in the United States of America.

To order additional copies of this book, contact:
Xlibris Corporation
1-888-795-4274
www.Xlibris.com
Orders@Xlibris.com

Contents

Introduction --- 11

PART ONE
The Skulls

Chapter One
THE CHINESE SKULLS:
SUYAN AND XUI MIN 17

Chapter Two
THE BRAZILIAN SKULLS: CALENJO,
TOL-REMY-RAN, RELL & LOPA 24

Chapter Three
THE HEALING SKULLS: OMBE, MOLMEC & CHEIRON 32

Chapter Four
DIMENSIONAL TRANSITION SKULLS: RUPEL &
TOLTELCUL 41

Chapter Five
THE TRAVELING SKULLS: PORTAL DE LUZ &
MAHASAMATMAN 53

Chapter Six
OTHER CRYSTAL SKULL CUSTODIANS 62

Chapter Seven
HOW CRYSTAL SKULLS COMMUNICATE WITH US 85

Chapter Eight
THE SACRED SEVEN 101

Chapter Nine
CRYSTAL SKULLS &
THE UNIVERSAL LIGHT GRIDWORK 111

PART TWO
Taking Care of Crystal Skulls

Chapter Ten
CHOOSING A CRYSTAL SKULL 121

Chapter Eleven
CLEANSING, DEDICATING & TUNING 126

Chapter Twelve
THE RESPONSIBILITY OF
BEING A CRYSTAL SKULL CUSTODIAN 136

PART THREE
Working With Your Crystal Skull

Chapter Thirteen
SELF-HEALING, SELF-PROTECTION,
MEDITATION & DREAMWORK 143

Chapter Fourteen
HEALING & PROTECTION EXERCISES FOR OTHERS 153

Epilogue --- 159

The Mohs Scale of Hardness for Minerals ------------ 169

Relevant Contact Details ------------------------------ 171

Bibliography --- 177

DEDICATION

This book is dedicated to my first and, at this time, only grandchild. May her life be long and healthy, being filled with the blessings of love, peace and the company of good friends. Welcome, Linsey Rose, to the beautiful starship Earth!

"It is my experience that working with a crystal skull is a multi-dimensional journey of discovery, enlightenment and growth."

C. 'Ravenia' Todd

Introduction

For seventeen years, I have worked closely with the mineral kingdom, and I have learned to love and respect the rocks, crystals and gemstones that were birthed by the Earth Mother. I often refer to them as "our crystal cousins" because I believe a close connection exists between humans and minerals. I see the mineral kingdom as the first extension of Divinity that came into being within this planet. As such, all minerals originally vibrated at a frequency that was similar to that of the Divine. They provided the building blocks for the later arrivals on Earth of plants, animals and, eventually, human beings. Minerals continue to lend their support, but working in proximity with us can alter their energy vibrations. Therefore, it is my belief that we must ensure their properties are only utilized for pure objectives and with good intentions. Also, I do not believe we can ever truly own minerals. Like children, they come into our keeping to be cared for and watched over. In this way, we are their custodians, but not their owners.

In my experience, mineral specimens that have been left in their original form and those that man has reshaped, all work on an individual basis with each one of us. Many books have been written expounding the various properties of this agate or that feldspar. However, I have found that too much generalization belittles the amazing ability a mineral has to attune itself to the specific needs of whomsoever is caring for it. Consequently, this book not only tells the reader about my encounters with crystal skulls, but also includes other people's impressions and experiences with these facilitators of healing and soul progression.

I am aware that some people believe only the ancient crystal skulls are worthy of merit, and those that were carved in recent years are merely inferior copies with no special attributes or abilities. However, from my own experiences and those of other people, I would argue that contemporary crystal skulls have much to offer us. I appreciate there is no mystery surrounding their origin or purpose, as with some of the old and ancient skulls. Also, it is usually possible to learn who carved a modern day crystal skull. Nevertheless, I think all crystal skulls hold a great deal of information within them that they are happy to share with us, if we are willing to work with them in a framework of love and respect.

The medium from which they were fashioned is extremely ancient, dating back to a time when our planet was very young. The primordial elements, which helped in the creation of minerals, have witnessed the progression of Earth from her long ago beginnings to her present-day existence. Human beings are merely a transient species compared to the mineral kingdom. Minerals were here eons before us and they will remain long after our demise. So it seems logical they would have plenty to teach us, whether they were carved into a specific shape in ancient times or just yesterday. Obviously, the energy of the carver is imprinted within the skull, as is the vibrational potency of the location from which the mineral was mined. These factors hold true for both ancient and contemporary crystal skulls.

The stories that accompany some of the ancient skulls are much more intriguing than what can be said about those that were recently created. The origin of these artifacts is linked with Atlantis or even further back in time. Some people believe they were brought to that lost continent from outer space or possibly another dimension of reality. In later times, it is known that the Mayans and the Aztecs used them within sacred ceremonies.

Some, it is thought, remain undiscovered, being buried in various parts of the world, such as, the Americas and Tibet. The Native Americans believe that among those yet to be unearthed are twelve companions to the intriguing Mitchell-Hedges Skull. When all thirteen skulls reunite, they say the outcome will be truly illuminating. This crystal skull was discovered by Anna Mitchell-Hedges in 1924 in what was British Honduras and is now known as Belize. Anna is the adopted daughter of Frederick Mitchell-Hedges and had accompanied him on an exploration of a lost Mayan city named Lubaantun. On the day of her seventeenth birthday, she saw something glinting in the sunlight, and when the rubble covering the object was eventually removed, the upper section of this crystal skull was revealed. The lower jaw was discovered some time later. When scientifically examined in 1970, this artifact showed no signs of having been hand or machine carved. Over the years, there have been several speculations about its age, who created it and how it was formed. Whatever its true origin, the Mitchell-Hedges Skull, including the movable lower jaw, was created from one magnificent, clear quartz specimen.

The places of origin for many contemporary crystal skulls are Brazil, Mexico, China, Europe and North America. Although they do not carry with them tales of belonging to lost continents or of being relics of a bygone civilization, many of them are being used for healing and spiritual purposes. In my opinion, this gives these skulls a very special quality that will greatly enhance with time and further usage.

There are doubts about the authenticity of some ancient crystal skulls. It is possible that several of them were carved in Europe in the second half of the nineteenth century and then proffered as Mayan and Aztec artifacts. However, just as I have stated for the modern day crystal skulls, I am certain these supposedly ancient ones have much wisdom to share with us.

Many people think the image or likeness of a skull represents death, therefore, even those created from crystals are disliked or even feared. They are looked upon as the harbingers of ill fortune. I do not feel this way about them. To me, a crystal skull symbolizes the truth that death is just a transition to another level of consciousness. The carving process, which the mineral specimen has undergone, changed it into a new form. Similarly, the experience of physical death is our metamorphosis into beings of spirit. I also believe crystal skulls lovingly remind us that just as they have been carved from a lasting medium, our true essence was also fashioned from something eternal.

Light-filled Blessings
November 28, 2000
(Waxing Moon in Capricorn)

PART ONE

The Skulls

Chapter One

THE CHINESE SKULLS: SUYAN AND XUI MIN

Although I had read about the Mitchell-Hedges Skull many years ago, my real introduction to crystal skulls happened in 1997. I was working at the Mind Body Spirit Festival in London, England, helping a very good friend sell crystals and gemstone jewelry. This was not the only year I worked on his stand, but it was the first time he had several crystal skulls on display. They were of different sizes, carved from a fine quality, Russian clear quartz. They were true works of art. My friend always encouraged me to "play with the crystals" and on this occasion he invited me to hold one of the skulls. I remember that a feeling of true reverence came over me as he placed the skull in my hands. Its clarity and polish were superb and I could sense that its energy was most profound. I only held it for a few moments because I received the impression that I was holding something very sacred. I almost felt unworthy to maintain contact with it. As

I recall the experience now, I am sure I was not ready at that time to work with the higher vibrations of a crystal skull.

One year later, at the same holistic festival, I purchased two fluorite skulls that had been carved in China. It was May 1998, and this date has taken on great significance within my life because during that month, I began to suffer from a rare illness known as Transverse Myelitis. In layman's terms it is a lesion on the spinal cord caused by inflammation, and its effects can be very devastating. Depending on the location of the lesion, some or a greater part of the body and its functions can be dramatically impaired. For me the inflammation was cited at the level of the lower four thoracic vertebrae, and this caused increasing numbness and loss of strength and sensory input from the waist down. Ultimately, I became paralyzed within the lower half of my body and I was confined to a wheelchair for a short period of time.

My reason for writing about this illness is to illustrate a point that I would like to make about crystal skulls. They do not come into our keeping haphazardly, there is purpose and order within their arrival. At times of great change within our personal lives, one or more crystal skulls will possibly make an appearance in order to assist with the process. Sometimes, they will be the initiators of those changes for us. The onset of Transverse Myelitis radically altered my day-to-day existence in a number of ways. I had to abandon my professional career and take early retirement due to ill health. My workaholic attitude towards life was also abruptly brought to a standstill. I changed from working full time every weekday and teaching on many weekends, to being confined to a couch. There I could either watch TV or read a book.

However, life has taught me that even though this type of change can be very difficult to accept, it always brings with it some compensations. For me, an inability to return to my professional work gave me the free time to pursue other avenues of interest. One of these was to begin to learn about ancient and contemporary crystal skulls. Another was a pursuit I had wanted to follow for many years. There was now time for me to write.

Both of these skulls that I bought in 1998 have remained in my possession. They were not carved from a high grade fluorite, nevertheless they have become very special to me. They are similar to one another, each weighing almost 1 lb. and being roughly the size of an apple. Like most Chinese fluorite, their colors are green and mauve. One has a band of mauve across the brow, continuing down through part of the right eye socket and completely through the left socket. The other has a stripe of mauve that zigzags from the back of the cranium, across the top and all the way down through the left eye socket to the lower jaw. This skull also has what is known as rainbow irising, which means rainbows of color can be seen when light hits some of the facets within the internal structure of certain mineral specimens. When I first bought the skulls, they were cloudy in appearance, but over time they have become more clear. It was evident that another mineral was enclosed within them, I could see white dots here and there on the surfaces. As it became easier to view the inside of the skulls, the dots proved to be the tips of tiny, calcite crystals embedded within the fluorite.

The skulls were placed in the spare bedroom of my London apartment along with many other crystals. This was not the only room that housed my mineral friends because they have always been on display in every area of my home. As time passed and while I remained mobile, I frequently felt drawn towards the skulls. I would bring them into my living room and just sit holding one or the other. While doing this one day, I suddenly knew that the skull I was holding, the one with the rainbow irising, had a name. At the same time, I was becoming aware that all crystal skulls have names by which we can know them. The name I was given was Suyan. I then held the other skull, asked for its name, and was told it was Xui Min.

From that time onwards, I began to understand certain facts about crystal skulls just by sitting quietly with one and 'tuning into' the information it was sharing with me. I learned that each skull, in fact, has many names, but will give to its custodian the one that is right for that person. This has everything to do with the vibration of the name. Its frequency will initiate the work the skull will do with, and for, its human friend. Some names are ordinary, everyday and familiar, while others are very different, being hyphenated or having unusual spelling. I was also told that each skull possesses an energy signature or vibration that can be considered male/projective, or female/receptive, or androgynous/projective and receptive. However, later research has shown me that these energy signatures can change from time to time. This has led me to believe that the true energy vibration of crystal skulls is androgynous, but that they present themselves to us as male, female, or androgynous, depending on what is best for each of us.

Further work with the two Chinese skulls gave me Suyan's energy signature as receptive. She brings healing, particularly to the etheric body, which is almost like a second skin to the physical body. She has also proved helpful with meditations. Xui Min's energy vibration was given as projective and he is a protective skull. This protection is essential for journeys beyond the physical, such as, out-of-body experiences and the dream state. He has told me he can also be used as a tool for scrying, which is commonly known as "crystal gazing," but this is not a pursuit of mine.

The percentage of people, who regain good mobility after developing Transverse Myelitis, is very small. Many remain in a wheelchair with a greater or lesser degree of paralysis. They can also suffer from severe bladder and bowel dysfunction for the rest of their lives. To date, there is no medical cure for this neurological problem. Given time, the body does or, more frequently, does not heal itself. Knowing this, I consider myself to be truly blessed because I was able to learn how to stand and walk, again, albeit more slowly than before. Learning to walk as an adult is a humbling experience. We do not retain memories of learning this skill during infancy. However, a determined attitude and a good sense of humor can help make the process possible a second time around.

The damage to nerves and nerve endings, caused by the lesion, has left a legacy of numbness, hypersensitivity, stiffness and pain in my legs and feet. I am unable to stoop down or kneel, and sitting down in the bathtub is a fun project. However, the things I can do far outweigh those that I can no longer achieve, and I believe my two fluorite skulls helped with my recovery. From the very first day that I woke up with numbness in my left hip, my husband gave me Reiki, a form of 'hands-on' healing, and I was also taking certain essences within the range of the Bach Flower Remedies. I am convinced these two therapies helped me to combat this illness, but I believe it was Suyan and Xui Min who ultimately put me back on my feet.

During the first weeks of my recovery and after I had returned home from the hospital, I found it very difficult to remain asleep at night. There was only one position in which I could lie, and that was on my right side with a pillow between my legs. Within about an hour of falling asleep, I would wake up with extreme pain and stiffness in my legs, and they would also feel quite cold from a lack of circulation. This discomfort could only be relieved by movement, therefore, I would get up and hobble about, leaning heavily on my Zimmer frame. Throughout each night, I would need to repeat this exercise at hourly intervals. Obviously, this problem was proving to be a disturbance for my husband, who always has to rise very early for work, and so, I made a decision to sleep in the spare bedroom.

Whenever a disease or accident causes immobility, the

relevant muscles begin to atrophy. Therefore, I was given a program of intensive, daily physio-therapy, even before I left the hospital, and this continued for a number of weeks after I returned home. It soon became apparent that the strength was returning to my limbs, and my physio-therapist was astounded by my progress. She remarked that she had never seen anyone recover so quickly. I was certain my improvement was due to the Reiki and the Bach Flower Remedies, together with some help from my angelic guides. However, one night after a session of stumbling around in order to ease the stiffness and pain, I went back to my bed and waited for sleep to return. Suddenly my attention was drawn to the two fluorite skulls that were on a shelf a few feet away from the bed. Due to my previous inability to move around my home and my subsequent hospitalization, I had completely forgotten that they were there. Yet at that moment I became acutely aware of their presence. It was almost as though they were calling to me and, although it was dark in the room, I could vaguely see them. Having caught my attention, they then made me aware that they were responsible for my rapid recovery. I did not hear voices telling me this information, it was just an inner knowing. Each night as I slept, they were bringing both healing and protection to my etheric body and this was reflected, in turn, into my physical body. I suddenly knew it was no accident that I was sleeping in the room with them, it had been arranged to happen that way. I also received the impression that it was important for me to continue sleeping close to them in order for their healing work to be maintained. I did, in fact, remain in that room at night for several weeks after I was discharged from the physio-therapy clinic.

Previous experience with the mineral kingdom had taught me to always show gratitude to any crystal with which I was working, and the skulls were no exception to this rule. As I became more mobile, I frequently went into the spare bedroom during the daytime and said a "thank you" to them, as I gently stroked the top of each skull. To some people this may appear to be an odd practice, but I truly love my crystals, no matter what shape or size they may be. To me they are almost as precious as my family and my dearest friends. In my experience, if we treat the mineral, plant and animal kingdoms with as much genuine love and caring as we need for ourselves, then many blessings come to us.

During the time since my recovery from Transverse Myelitis, I have not done any specific work with Suyan and Xui Min. In December 1999, when we sold our apartment and bought a house in Kent, all of our crystals and mineral specimens were packed away in bubble wrap. After our move, these two skulls and a number of other crystals remained packed in their boxes. In previous years, this had also happened to certain crystals following other house moves. This was partly due to convenience, but I have also learned that when I feel reluctant to unpack a crystal, it is because it is telling me that it requires a rest. To keep a crystal wrapped up and in darkness is somewhat like returning it to its place of birth, the inner levels of our planet. Sometimes, I have left crystals packed away for more than a year and, at other times, it has only been for several weeks. Either way, whenever I feel prompted to unpack them, I know it is because they are fully rested and refreshed and are ready to work with me, again.

As soon as I began writing this book, I became aware that Suyan and Xui Min were asking me to bring them back out of their bubble wrap. This I did, and whenever I sit typing, they are close by on my computer desk because I feel this is where they want to be. I believe they are watching over my work and guiding me through the process of telling others about crystal skulls.

Chapter Two

THE BRAZILIAN SKULLS: CALENJO, TOL-REMY-RAN, RELL & LOPA

I would like to give a word of caution to anyone who is contemplating purchasing a crystal skull. These mineral carvings appear to enjoy each other's company. Therefore, if you acquire one, more will undoubtedly follow! I was not aware of this fact when I purchased the fluorite skulls, but given time it has held true for me. Other people have also reported a similar occurrence after their first crystal skull came to live with them.

My family of crystal skulls began to grow in November of 1998, when my husband and I decided to buy two skulls as Christmas presents for each other. We located a retailer in the USA who was selling fine quality, Brazilian crystal skulls. These were fashioned from such minerals as clear quartz, smoky quartz, citrine and rose quartz. Their measurements ranged from no larger than a walnut to the size of a newborn's skull. For my husband, I chose a skull that was carved from an extremely clear specimen of smoky quartz. Its size is that of a large plum, it has excellent polish and was formed by superb craftsmanship. On the top right-hand side of this skull is an extensive rainbow irising area that is truly wonderful. Calenjo is his name and he gave his energy signature as projective. I believe this particular skull is very special, but I have yet to gain any further information from him. Perhaps this is because he is my husband's crystal companion or maybe his radiance prevents me from working with him. Whenever I hold him, I become lost in his exquisite clarity and form.

My husband chose a citrine skull for me. Once again, the carving and polish are of a superior quality and this skull has also presented a projective vibration. He is slightly larger than Calenjo and is known as Tol-Remy-Ran. There is a light, wispy veil running vertically and midway between the front and back of the skull. Veils are fascinating patterns within the internal structure of quartz that resemble galaxies, when seen from a great distance in space. Tol-Remy-Ran also has areas of rainbow irising behind the jaw, at the base of the skull and behind the eye sockets.

Since this mineral friend came into my keeping, I have learned a number of interesting facts from him about crystal skulls. Our human skulls house and protect our brains, which can be considered storehouses of knowledge. Similarly, all skulls created from minerals hold and guard Earth's ancient history and the lost technology belonging to the sunken continents of Mu and Atlantis. The blueprint for our future is also hidden inside them. The vast majority of the human brain's potential is not yet understood or used. Similarly, the full abilities and functions of crystal skulls have not yet been revealed to us. At this present time, we are not sufficiently developed nor ready to use this awesome power in a responsible and loving manner.

Tol-Remy-Ran also divulged one of the reasons why mineral specimens were fashioned long ago into the shape of skulls. It was to create a hidden message for future generations. Perhaps the ancients knew that over the passage of time we would forget how interconnected we are with our planet. When we ignore this fact, as has happened since the industrial revolution, we ravage our Earth and eliminate increasing numbers of plant and animal life. Ultimately, this process of elimination will embrace us, as well. The crystal skull's message is not difficult to understand. It tells us of our affinity with Earth by reminding us that minerals are an innate part of both us and our planet. A crystal skull is a mineral carving, a human skull contains minerals within its form. If we think of ourselves as something totally separate from the planet, then it becomes much easier for us to abuse her. When we understand our close connection, we cherish and respect her.

I have learned from this informative crystal friend that the Mitchell-Hedges Skull holds within it the location details of the other twelve, similar crystal skulls. However, this ancient artifact has imparted very little of its vast store of wisdom to anyone at the present time. Apparently, it is waiting for the planet's progression and the right person to activate its work. While on the subject of ancient crystal skulls, Tol-Remy-Ran indicated that contemporary skulls can acquire some of the properties of their ancient counterparts, if they are placed within close proximity to them for a period of time. It is as though the old ones teach the new skulls what they know.

In addition to what he has shared about ancient and modern day crystal skulls, Tol-Remy-Ran has led me into a number of interesting meditations and given me some techniques to promote self-healing, protection and distant healing. These procedures are discussed later in this book.

By February 1999, both I and my husband were fully

intrigued by crystal skulls and we were ready to welcome more into our home. We ordered another four from the same US company and eagerly awaited their arrival. They varied in size from that of a golf ball to the equivalent of a newborn's skull. The two larger ones are not discussed in this chapter, but are detailed in Chapter Three. The other two were carved from smoky and clear quartz, and I quickly learned their names as being Rell and Lopa, soon after their arrival.

Rell is a high grade, clear quartz skull. She is golf ball-size and presents a receptive energy signature. Both her clarity and polish are excellent and there is a small area of rainbow irising towards the left-hand base of the cranium. She was originally bought to be passed on to someone else, but she quickly endeared herself to me. Whenever I hold her, I begin to smile and feel cheerful. I speak of her as "a sweet little skull."

In 1999, I and a very good friend conducted several home blessings for various people. These are a form of spiritual treatment for houses and apartments that require the removal of any unwanted, left-over energies from previous owners and tenants. They also dispel any spirit attachments and promote positivity and harmony within the home. We used space clearing techniques and the power of crystals to cleanse each home, then gave some Feng Shui tips to help maintain a positive atmosphere. Soon after Rell arrived, it became clear to me that she wanted to be a part of these home blessings.

As soon as we arrived at a house or apartment, I set up a temporary altar on a table, and this was the focal point from which we worked throughout the home. I laid a special cloth on the table, then lit incense and a candle and, finally, set out our space clearing tools. We asked the person living in the home to pick an angel card so that the chosen angelic quality would work with us during the home blessing. Once Rell became a part of the process, she was placed on the altar and, I believe, she oversaw and facilitated our work. One benefit

I definitely experienced from her presence was a heightened sense of whose energy presence was attached to the home. This was something I had previously been able to identify, but not with such ease and precision. Rell also gave a boost to my work of sending spirit attachments on their way to the higher realms.

I think of Rell as a Light tool because she has such an uplifting quality about her. This has proved true for me and for any souls that are trapped close to the physical plane. In contrast, Lopa is a very different mineral tool.

This is a smoky quartz skull with an androgynous vibration. It is of a similar size to Tol-Remy-Ran. Soon after its arrival, it introduced itself as Lopa, and this is the name by which I know it. However, much later within a dream, it gave me its full name, which is Caterguillopa. Even so, I continue to think of it as Lopa. There is further information about the dream in Chapter Seven. Lopa's color is a rich brown that is much darker than that of Calenjo and it was carved from a lesser grade of quartz. There are many veils and interesting structures within the entirety of Lopa, giving it a more solid appearance than most of my other crystal skulls.

When Lopa first arrived, I was very concerned about it because it was obvious to me that it was filled with negativity. Minerals can pick up negativity in all manner of ways, including from being used for evil purposes. Therefore, the kindest and wisest act we can do for them, when they first come to us, is to cleanse them. In my opinion, this is a rule that should always be followed, no matter from where they may have come. From time to time, certain mineral specimens that were in need of major cleansing have come into my possession. Lopa was one of these. Working as a crystal healing practitioner over a long period of time, has given me an astute sense of the degree of positive or negative energy within minerals. Eventually, this ability comes naturally to those who work closely with the mineral kingdom.

Two of my friends, who are lovers and collectors of crystals, were extremely suspicious of Lopa in the beginning. They would not touch this skull nor even go near it. However, after several weeks of being cleansed and shown plenty of love by me, Lopa began to greatly improve in their opinions. On seeing the skull sometime after her first encounter with it, the one friend was certain it was not Lopa. She thought the size, color and appearance were different and it took some time for me to convince her that it was the same crystal skull. The other friend felt quite drawn to Lopa when she saw it, again. She appeared to have completely forgotten how hesitant and wary she had felt about it several months before.

These incidents demonstrate just how important and powerful the act of cleansing can be. It is a procedure to remove any negative energy within the mineral specimen, and to ask that the negativity be transmuted to the Divine so that it may reach its highest, positive form. In simple terms, it is a ritual to recycle the mineral's energy. There are many different ways to cleanse crystals and crystal skulls, and this subject is addressed later in the book.

Apart from cleansing Lopa, I have also spent time just holding it and talking to it. It is a very powerful skull whose capabilities are immense. It has informed me that it can initiate out-of-body experiences and influence the dream state. In the beginning, it gave me the impression that it was as willing to work for evil as it was for good. Also, that it was not holding onto negative energy, but merely allowing it to pass through itself. Since then I have tried to impress upon it that by allowing negative energy into itself, much of that lower vibration had remained with it. I like to think that I have shown it the benefits of only being used positively, and I trust that its change in appearance reflects its acceptance of this. It displays many rainbows throughout itself, where there were none before, and there are areas of clarity that previously were cloudy.

However, I feel very strongly that Lopa is not a crystal skull for the uninitiated. As with a restored fallen angel, is there the possibility of falling, again? I do not know how Lopa became filled with negativity, but I think that it was used inappropriately at some time. It is unlikely that I will give this skull to anyone else, I have a sense of obligation to monitor how it will be used. I am also careful not to work with it when I am feeling anything other than completely well in mind, body and spirit.

I have sometimes held Lopa, when I am in bed, and I know it has affected my dreams. I believe it teaches me while I sleep, but, on waking, I cannot always recall what I have been given.

Together with most of my other crystal skulls, Calenjo, Tol-Remy-Ran, Rell and Lopa have made their home on my living room window-sill. They are spread out in a line and facing into the room. I have placed them together because this feels right, almost as though they need each other's company. On sunny days they enjoy several hours of basking in the sunlight that, in itself, is a form of cleansing. Suyan and Xui Min are not with these skulls because the colors of fluorite will fade when exposed to periods of direct sunlight. When not helping me with my writing, they are happy keeping each other company in a display case in my living room.

Although logical thinking tells me otherwise, there are times when it appears that one or more of the skulls have moved their positions slightly. Apparently, they adjust their placement by themselves for some unknown reason. I have no other explanation for this occurrence. Neither cats nor children are ever in my home. In addition, the skulls are not in a location where they could be accidentally bumped. I have considered the possibility that vibration from passing traffic could cause this movement. The bay windows of my living room face the street, but are a distance from it. However, other objects on the same window-sill of lesser weight than the crystal skulls do not move. Also, I had noticed this phenomenon previously, when they were housed on another window-sill in my London apartment, and those windows were well away from the road. To me this is just one more example of how amazing and extraordinary crystal skulls can be.

Chapter Three

THE HEALING SKULLS: OMBE, MOLMEC & CHEIRON

I believe all crystal skulls are tools for healing to some degree. As previously explained, both Suyan and Xui Min assisted in my recovery from Transverse Myelitis, but I do not think they would necessarily work in a healing capacity for everyone. Some crystal skulls, however, are most definitely healers. Their primary function is to initiate wellness in people and animals. Two such Brazilian skulls came into my home together with the arrival of Rell and Lopa.

Ombe was a pale citrine skull, weighing 1.25 lb. and presenting a projective energy signature. His polish and clarity were excellent, his carving was of a high standard and there were several areas of rainbow irising within him. After holding him on a couple of occasions, I began to realize that he would not remain with us, that he was actually for someone else. As if to confirm this, I channeled a message from him one day. It was given through automatic writing, which is a method of receiving information from the spirit realms and other dimensions. I had discovered that I could do this form of channeling a number of years earlier. Therefore, I was not surprised to feel prompted to get a pad and a pen in order to express Ombe's words. They were as follows:

> "I want to belong to someone who will cherish me and use my radiance for healing the little ones, the children, who are known to you as the animals. I am a worker, not a possession to be locked away for private contemplation. Not only will I heal the animals, but I will also aid their communication with humans and give humans an understanding of their animal companions.
>
> I can connect animals and humans in the manner they should be experiencing, the way they did once long ago. Souls and their fragments rejoin when I am brought into their proximity. Treat me gently and with respect as you would an animal. I am of their nature and humility. Oceans blue and purple peaks, I wish to return home."

The sentence referring to soul fragments can be interpreted in two different ways. In shamanism it is believed that as we experience traumas, illnesses and unhappy events, fragments of our souls break off. These broken pieces are then left behind and remain separate as we journey on through our lives. If a person visits a shaman to rectify this problem, a healing procedure known as "soul retrieval" will take place. Within this process, a shaman is able to journey to the dimensions where these fragments exist and, on behalf of the person, s/he will retrieve them and reconnect them to the main soul. Therefore, Ombe may have been saying that he can perform the act of soul retrieval, which is, most definitely, a form of healing.

However, many years ago one of my angelic guides gave me information on the souls of animals. Put very simply, animals possess a fragment soul as opposed to the more complex souls of humans. A full explanation of how this came to be can be found in my book *Soul Wisdom, Volume One*. Also, some animals may possess a fragment soul that on another level is actually a part of a person's Higher Self. This is the greater part of the soul that is not incarnated into the physical plane. In this circumstance, if the animal becomes that person's pet, a very close bond is formed and, at a higher level, rejoining takes place. If this is what Ombe meant, then presumably he can facilitate the rejoining.

Within a few weeks of his arrival, we met a young couple who owned a metaphysical store in Croydon. This town is within the southern boundary of the Greater London Area. When they saw Ombe, they were completely enthralled with him. They had recently returned from Mexico, where they had spent their honeymoon. Their reason for choosing that country was their search for a crystal skull. They felt compelled to acquire one of these mineral carvings and they knew there was a good possibility of finding one in Mexico. Unfortunately, any crystal skulls they saw there were too expensive for them to purchase, and they returned home very disappointed.

It quickly became obvious to both my husband and me that Ombe was the right skull for them. After negotiating a price that they could afford and one that did not leave us out-of-pocket, they became this skull's new owners. While chatting to the young woman before we parted company, she told me she was a healer, working particularly with animals. To me this was verification of something I truly believe, the fact that there are no coincidences. Ombe had definitely gone into the keeping of the right crystal skull custodian. Although life may often appear to be a set of random events, there is always order and purpose in the universe.

We planned to visit their store in Croydon at some point in the future, but summer vacation and plans for our move became a priority. However, about five months after the sale of Ombe and while we were going through the process of selling our apartment and buying our next home, I received what, I believe, was follow-up news about them. A student, who had taken training with me at an adult education college in London, came to visit me. She noticed the row of crystal skulls on my window-sill and she began to ask questions about them. She wanted to know if I believed they talked to me. I assured her that crazy as it might seem, I was positive they were able to do this. She then explained that the owners of her "most favorite" store, where she had bought many crystals, were moving to Glastonbury in Somerset. According to her, they said they were told to do this by their crystal skull. When she added that their store was in Croydon, I asked for the name of it and, of course, it was the same one the young couple owned. I have not been able to confirm whether they moved to Glastonbury, but I am presuming they did because their store is no longer in Croydon. There is an ever-growing metaphysical community in Glastonbury, and I can imagine that Ombe would feel very much at home in what was once a part of the mystical Isle of Avalon.

* * *

Molmec is the fourth crystal skull that we bought in February 1999. He gives a projective energy signature and weighs 1.60 lb. He has fine clarity and polish, was carved with good precision from clear quartz, and has a number of veils towards the back of the cranium and behind the eye sockets. He also displays several faceted structures within him that reflect back light in a myriad of rainbows.

When Molmec gave me his name, he announced that he is a healing skull who primarily brings healings to groups rather than to individuals. I feel he did proclaim rather than just tell me this fact because there is nothing humble about him. He appears to be proud, but not arrogant, and he is often quite bossy. He has made it obvious on a number of occasions that he needs to accompany me when I give workshops about crystals, crystal skulls and healing modalities. These workshops usually take place at holistic festivals and health shows, also at the London adult education college about which I previously wrote. I made a black velvet cushion for Molmec at his request and he rests on this, on a table in front of the participants, when I am teaching.

Towards the end of these workshops, I usually lead a short healing meditation. At the beginning of this procedure, I ask the participants to request that they only receive what is right and appropriate for them at that time. Then they close their eyes and sit quietly. During the minutes of the meditation, I believe Molmec channels and focuses healing energy towards each one of them. I have seen energy emanating from him and connecting with various people within a group. I have also observed that the immediate space surrounding Molmec takes on a similar effect to what can be seen when heat, which is rising from something, distorts the air above it. The healing that Molmec gives may take place on any one, or a combination, of the physical, the emotional, the mental and the spiritual levels.

I have received feedback from some of the people who experienced these healing sessions with Molmec. The majority of them reported feeling a very powerful energy passing through them. One student from the college contacted me several days later to report that she was feeling greatly affected by the healing meditation, both emotionally and physically. She added that although what she was experiencing was almost traumatic, she was sure she was being made to address problems that required attention. She said she knew it was what she needed, but that it was also very difficult to undergo.

On another occasion, while giving a lecture about crystal skulls, an elderly woman became very excited at the end of the healing meditation. She then explained that she had suffered from crippling and painful arthritis for a number of years. During the session, she felt energy coming to her from Molmec. It entered her head and moved right through her whole skeletal structure, changing the composition of her bones for several minutes. She described the experience as being "powerful and beautiful," her skeleton became clear quartz for a time. She believed this process had strengthened her bones and lessened the adverse effects of the arthritis. I cannot be positive that she experienced a healing, but I am certain that as she left at the end of the lecture, she was walking more upright and far more sprightly than when she had arrived. Similarly, following another group healing meditation with Molmec, a woman told me her whole body became clear quartz during the session.

Molmec also participates in my distant healing sessions. I have been conducting these for a number of years and they are now enhanced by his presence. They usually take place early on weekend mornings and are a combination of distant healing with Reiki and the Tree of Light healing. The latter was formulated by Denise Linn, the well-known, metaphysical author and presenter. I received induction into this form of healing in 1992, while attending one of her Native American Spirituality courses. During a session, I sit quietly and hold Molmec on my lap. I then send the appropriate Reiki symbols to the recipients and perform the Tree of Light visualization. I believe Molmec intensifies, focuses and generally strengthens the whole process.

During each session, there are several people to whom I am sending the distant healing. They may have requested this themselves or someone has done so on their behalf. I include them on each occasion until such time as I am informed that it is no longer necessary. In my years of experience as a healing practitioner, I have found distant healing to be more powerful than 'hands-on' healing. Now, with the addition of Molmec's energy, the results are truly rewarding.

On August 11, 1999, there was a total eclipse of the sun that was well visible in the southern counties of England. I was at home on that day and, once it had begun, I lit a candle and some incense. I then felt the need to sit quietly and, as I did so, I received the impression that Molmec wanted to be with me. All of my crystal skulls were resting on the window-sill, so they did experience the energy of this special event. However, Molmec was held by me through the dimming of the sun and the following twilight. The energy of this eclipse felt very different from when the light begins to fade as night approaches or when very heavy, rain clouds move in and visibility becomes poor. There was an ethereal quality about it. It felt special and unusual, but not frightening.

After the sunlight returned and for the rest of that day, there was an almost tangible quality of exhilaration in the air. Molmec also seemed to be affected by the eclipse. New rainbows appeared in his depths and there were several, light blue patches of color inside him. By the end of the day, the blue patches had faded, but the rainbows have remained. I like to think the energy of this total eclipse added to Molmec's healing properties.

* * *

In the early spring of 2001, my husband and I visited a mineral warehouse in the north of England. We went there specifically to purchase some crystal skulls, and this we did. The minerals for these carvings come from all over the world, but the owner of the warehouse sends them to China to be fashioned into skulls, spheres, obelisks, etc. While we were making our choices, I noticed a clear quartz skull that was very cloudy and greatly in need of a cleansing. When I held this skull, I felt sadness and a strong sense of neglect coming from it. Although it weighs about 3.50 lbs., its price was quite inexpensive, presumably due to its appearance. Knowing that I could work with it and, hopefully, improve its condition, I decided to buy it.

When I unpacked the skull at home, a closer inspection of it revealed what appeared to be many tiny nicks across its cranium. However, these were not the result of damage, but were the exposed tips of facets within the mineral. When a crystal has these internal structures and is being carved into a shape, it requires first class polishing to remove such indentations. Seeing them was like déjà-vu, I had been shown a crystal skull with very similar markings in a dream the previous night. The full details of this dream are related in Chapter Seven. The name that was given to me for the dream skull was Cheiron and, when I asked for the name of this skull with the cloudy, neglected appearance, it was the same.

Cheiron is the archaic spelling for the Greek god Chiron, the king of the Centaurs, who was also a teacher, a healer and a warrior. He is sometimes referred to as "the wounded healer" because he was poisoned, but could not die. Being immortal, he had to endure pain and agony from the poison without the ultimate release that death brings.

I gave several cleansings to Cheiron and then left it on a sunny window-sill, where I felt it could recuperate. I did not attempt to do any work with this skull, but frequently held it and also took it into bed with me on several occasions. It gave me its energy vibration as androgynous.

After a short while, the right side of Cheiron began to clear and, over time, the cloudiness has diminished until there is only a small patch on the left-hand side. I have also observed that the majority of the indentations have disappeared, as though an invisible hand polished the cranium to a greater smoothness.

A couple of months after buying Cheiron, I was told that it is a healing skull, but specifically to help the terminally ill pass over into the spirit world. I did not gain this information from the skull, but from a friend named Samantha Elliott, who likes to be called Sam. In Chapter Seven, I explain how she is able to discern the spiritual and healing properties of crystal skulls. Three days before I was given this information, I had been asked to send distant healing to a woman in New York who was terminally ill with cancer. When Sam told me the work Cheiron would do, I knew her explanation was very timely.

The next morning I conducted a distant healing session specifically for the woman, using the help of Cheiron instead of having Molmec's assistance. Two days later, I learned that the woman had passed into spirit about thirty-six hours after I had performed the distant healing. She had been given several weeks to live, but I feel sure Cheiron quickly led her to the place where her suffering could end.

Over the years, I have been asked to send healing to several people who were not expected to recover from their illnesses. Now that Cheiron has arrived to help with this work, I know this skull's special energy will assist their journey to what one of my angelic guides calls "true reality."

Chapter Four

DIMENSIONAL TRANSITION SKULLS: RUPEL & TOLTELCUL

During the last quarter of the twentieth century, there were many warnings that humans need to change their ways or they will be doomed to extinction. Some of these cautions were given within channeled messages from spirit guides and the angelic realms. They indicate that life, as we know it, will disappear as a result of drastic climatic changes, caused by an axis shift, or a nuclear winter, or the greenhouse effect. The Earth Mother will rid herself of the vast majority of her human population and the few, who remain, will become the predecessors of a more compassionate and spiritually-minded human species. Other channelings speak of subtle changes in which humans progress from a third-dimensional existence to that of the fourth or even fifth. Whether these transformations will manifest as a result of physical events or due to higher dimensional evolution, these happenings are often referred to as the "Earth Changes" or "Dimensional Transitions."

Diane Stein's book *Prophetic Visions of the Future* takes a broad and in-depth look at these predicted changes. She has compiled relevant information from several sources in order to present a thought provoking image of Earth's future. Some of the predictions included in her book came from one of my angelic guides. Within my own book *Soul Wisdom, Volume One*, I have devoted a chapter to the Earth Changes and the channeled messages I have received about what lies ahead for us.

Even though I had been aware of these forecasts for a number of years, they were far from my thoughts when two new Brazilian crystal skulls arrived in the early summer of 1999. One of these skulls soon gave me his name as Toltelcul. He was carved from AAA grade rose quartz and presents a projective energy signature. This skull is a very pale pink color with excellent clarity, and is the size of a small plum. Apart from learning his name and vibration, I was not given anything further about him until I began to work with the second skull. Its energy signature is androgynous and it is the same size as Molmec. Carved from a very pale citrine, the skull has good clarity and plenty of rainbow irising in the lower jaw and throughout the cranium. Although my husband had laid claim to this crystal skull, I also felt quite drawn to it.

While holding the skull one day in late June of 1999, I received the impression that it wanted to give me some information through automatic writing. I found a notepad and a pen and wrote out a communication from an apparent collective consciousness. I believe the message is self-explanatory:

"If you work with the Voladi, you become changed. You understand unknown things, you fight for our cause, you are with us. We bring you the blossoming and the intent, we give you our solari. We create a new way of life for you, we are your companions and your gentle lords. Ours is the way of knowing, being and fulfillment. Across the stars we have come to be with you and we will remain in your domains because you are our cherished one. We were created to guide your kind to a higher evolvement, that of luminosity. Unlock our secrets and you will be forever changed. Keep us close, care for us, love us, as we do these things for you. Channel our words, our deeds, our thoughts, be our maiden of devotion. Conjure our essence into your being and we will restructure you for what is to come. Sleep with us, dream with us, spend your days with us. We will hold you close and guard you against all evil. We are the warriors of the Divine One, we possess all knowledge and understanding; and we wish to share it with you, for you will honor what we give to you and you will keep it sacred. I am Rupel of Alvera and I am now aligned with you and a part of you."

On the following day I channeled information on how to attune people to the higher vibrations of the Earth Changes. This message also came from the crystal skull that I began to think of as Rupel. I was given seven symbols, their names and a procedure, whereby five of the symbols build an etheric pyramid in which a participant is seated. The remaining two, together with one of the five, are then placed into the chakras and subtle bodies of that person. The latter are known as the etheric, the emotional, the lower mental, the higher mental, the intuitional, the spiritual and the divine. These bodies are usually represented as encircling, layer by layer, the physical body. Chakras are the energy centers that exist on the etheric body, but are connected to the physical body and all of the other subtle bodies.

When completed, the procedure realigns and attunes the recipient's DNA so that s/he is better able to integrate his/

her light body. During the process, Rupel oversees what is happening and I hold Toltelcul, as I was directed to do within the channeled message. Apparently, the actions that I perform, in order to construct the pyramid and to place the symbols within a person's subtle anatomy, have to pass through Toltelcul. He is the bridge between the physical level and that of the etheric.

In early July, the Voladi mentioned other crystal skulls. The first part of that message is reproduced here and the remainder is given in the Epilogue:

> "Guard the skull well, it will bring you much information. Other collectives also speak to humans through crystal skulls. The Max skull carries our vibration and allows us to accomplish healing work through its matrix. Similarly, the four skulls, which are buried in Tibet, have given great wisdom and healing to those who were able to be in their presence ..."

Max is considered to be one of the ancient crystal skulls whose healing abilities have become available to people in recent years. There is more information about this mineral carving in the following chapter. However, I have no knowledge of the Tibetan crystal skulls that are mentioned above.

I was intrigued by the DNA realignment/attunement procedure that Rupel had given and I was anxious to perform it for someone. The opportunity to do so was soon presented to me when I was invited to give a workshop at the August Festival of Holistic Living in London. This event takes place annually over the August Bank Holiday Weekend and I have been a guest speaker since 1996. In 1999 I decided to talk about the coming Earth Changes and to also conduct the procedure for the workshop participants.

As I worked through the process, it became obvious to me that it was very powerful and was affecting those present. One woman had brought her young baby with her and my attention was drawn to this child. He had been quiet throughout the workshop, being mostly asleep. However, he woke up as I began the procedure and remained very still and quiet with eyes wide open. It was as though he understood what was happening. At the end of the workshop, several people gave me feedback on what they had experienced. Some had felt physical reactions within their bodies, others were more affected on the emotional level. Without doubt, something had taken place during the process.

A year later and at the same festival, I repeated the workshop. Once again, both I and those who attended experienced the intensity and power of Rupel's procedure. I would like to have had further feedback on its long-term effects on the participants of either workshop. However, this has not been possible because I have no means of making contact with them.

Later, Rupel told me that this DNA realignment/attunement could also be conducted etherically. In other words, I could perform the procedure for someone, even if s/he was not present. The realignment and attunement would be passed to the recipient via the etheric level. Knowing how effective and powerful it can be to send distant healing at that level to others, I was very interested in attempting this new procedure at a distance.

At that time, September 1999, I was a member of an online list of people, who were interested in esoteric matters and who kept contact with each other by sending emails. I decided to offer Rupel's gift to anyone on the list who would like to receive it. To my surprise about twenty list members responded. They were from the US, the UK, Australia and Denmark. I conducted the procedure and then asked for feedback via email. Almost everyone responded and they all had experienced something during the session and afterwards. At the time of writing this book, I no longer have the email addresses for the majority of these people. However, for the three with whom I have remained in contact, I am including their original remarks below, as well as their more recent feedback, following my request for same. Each person appears to have benefited from the DNA realignment/attunement.

One of the recipients was a Hawaiian woman named Fay Pohaikawahine Graef, who presently lives in Citrus Heights, California. She is particularly interested in the ancient traditions of her people and their possible connection to the lost continent of Mu. Fay explained what happened during the procedure:

"... Anyway, I woke up at exactly 2:30a.m. California time and felt included. Early in the morning (after going back to sleep) I also started having very vivid dreams (these started yesterday, but are getting stronger) of a hole with water flowing in from all sides, great masses of water into which I jump, flowing in great spirals, downward. Sometimes the spirals are water, sometimes the spirals take on the form of snakes (very flat snakes). Also, there is a small ball floating in the air with a long filament attached—I know this to be the center of the earth. It is all very peaceful and this morning I feel great. Thought I'd give you some feedback on what is happening. With love and aloha, Fay."

In a recent email, Fay expressed how, she believes, the procedure has affected her life:

"... I do know that over the past two years many things have come together more clearly in my mind, ancient connections and links that I have searched for, for over 20 years. They seem to be flowing in like that hole with water flowing in from all sides. I have finally found a place of comfort in sharing these connections with others, freely and without reservation. I feel a great sense of peace and balance . . . he hawai'i au, Fay."

Marc Edwards was another member of the online list who accepted my offer. Marc lives in New York and is a jazz musician. He plays drums and percussion, and can be found listed in several jazz reference books. Marc is also a Reiki Master and is interested in metaphysics. His information on what he experienced is thought provoking because it suggests that the effects can be felt before the process takes place within the physical level:

"Last night, I experienced lots of inner wakefulness—much more than usual. Although my body was resting, sleeping if you will, mentally, I was wide awake. When I got up, the clock showed 2:56a.m. EST. I thought to myself, "I guess Maz has finished doing the attunement."

Two days before you actually did the attunement, I began experiencing heat in the middle of my chest. Sometimes, it's closer to my heart. The heat is so intense, it feels as if I am radiating energy, similar to a hot stove. Could it be that my heart chakra is opening? I can't tell. Usually one experiences love for his fellow man when that happens. I'm not getting that—just the sensation of heat radiating outward, nonstop. There is no physical pain or discomfort. My attention is constantly drawn to my chest."

"Maz" is a name by which many people know me. Contact with Marc through email, while writing this chapter, has confirmed my belief that Rupel's procedure is an aid to our spiritual progression:

> "After Maz worked her magic on yours truly, I didn't give the attunement a second thought. The physical sensations did eventually subside. Gradually, over the weeks and months, I began to notice my attention shifting from material concerns to those of a more spiritual nature. Although I'm a long term TM meditator, I also do the yoga workout with Steve Ross and his students on 'Inhale.' The show airs during the week on the Oxygen Channel. Reiki is another modality that I find useful. All of these disciplines are tools designed to help me accomplish my mission.
> The events of September 11, 2001 has had the effect of pushing me deeper into these practices. I look forward to each day, knowing that I'm getting closer to achieving my goals, both material and spiritual. Thank you Maz."

The third online list person, who has given me feedback on the procedure, is Yolanda Badillo. She is a young woman and, like Marc Edwards, lives in New York. She works as a hairdresser and beautician and has a son who is 3 years old. Even though her life is extremely busy, she is following a spiritual path. Yolanda emailed me with the following information soon after she received the etheric DNA realignment/attunement:

> "I felt the energy, since before I went to bed, was very sensitive. The next day I was extremely relaxed, so relaxed I wanted to sleep more, but it was impossible to accomplish. I felt my heart open up more each time I meditated. Would like to know if you can include me two more times in the process so it can be a trinity process for myself? I greatly

appreciate all you're doing and thank you very much from my heart. May the universal light be in you, with you, and in your spirit . . ."

Following Yolanda's request to undergo the process, again, on two further occasions, I included her in a second round of this procedure. This happened a few days after the first and was as a consequence of other list members asking me to realign them. The original recipients had posted positive remarks to the group about what they had experienced. This encouraged others to request it. Later, I also conducted this procedure a third time for Yolanda. Below are parts of the two separate emails she sent, telling me about her impressions after the second and third sessions:

" . . . I slept all morning, practically, in between of cracking my eyes open at intervals that were very small, to see what he (her son) was up to. I rested and had a pretty great day. Very balanced and still in the sense of calmness. Will see if the attunement will help with balancing all my levels for better groundedness, as well as inner peace and power. For the stillness I can see what will be ahead of it and respond appropriately, not react to it. Thank you so much and looking forward for the last one and waiting to see how it will affect me . . . Again, I wish to express my gratitude for your service to the people you have extended yourself to without really knowing us, but for one thing in common—the interest to better ourselves and get closer to God."

"This time I was charged with a lot of energy. I was up until past the time of initiation and have been very active, especially since we came back . . . My little boy contracted a virus on the trip and then an ear infection... So very little sleep since, but I am able to keep up at a better pace. Have had vivid dreams in the short spurts of sleep, but when my baby cries in discomfort and wakes me up, I loose the consciousness of the dreams. Again, many thanks, Yolanda"

I recently emailed Yolanda and asked her if she has had any positive effects from the three DNA realignments/attunements that she etherically received two years ago. This was her answer:

"I have become a much more stronger, loving individual. And I find myself much more willing to let people be who they are, as well as allow myself to be me. I have been through some very hard physical changes, medically. All gone practically now, and old stuff has been allowed to be released, as well, right now. I still feel I need some assistance in the recall so I can be better to serve. For I have memories of information, which I can't thoroughly process yet. Along with also letting go of people who have not served me well, in the way of being totally honest and present with their truth. I've learned to let people be, but won't accept being dragged with their dilemmas. When we are not honest with ourselves, then much disharmony arises. I can no longer do this dance for I have a strong family now with my child and his father... So I think that the process you so freely shared was quite a positive one for myself. There was some physical disturbances after, but I find it was all releasing and a hell of a lot of letting-go, so I can become who I'm supposed to be. Thank you."

Another woman, who asked to receive the procedure etherically, was Frances Engelhardt. I originally met Frances in the Fall of 1999, when I attuned her to the First Level of Elestial Reiki. Early in April 2000 and while she was living in London, Frances contacted me, made her request, and I performed the DNA realignment/attunement for her. However, I had no further contact with her until recently because she now spends most of her days in Greece. When I met with her, I explained about this book and asked her to give me some feedback on the procedure that she had undergone nineteen months earlier. The following comments are what she gave to me:

> "I was very excited when I read about Marion's attunements from a crystal skull. I understood it raised our energy vibrations, which I understood to be cleansing and a move towards 'light beingness.' And being a novice at all of this, I thought it was an amazing concept to have received this information from the mineral kingdom. I called Marion, having no idea that the attunements could be given etherically. She explained when she wanted to do it, which was early morning around 7:00a.m., and that I may wake up. Sure enough, at 7:00a.m. on the day I received the attunement, I woke up from a deep sleep. I can remember feeling excited about having received it and having a feeling of "walking on sunshine" that day.
>
> Major shifts have happened in my life since that time. A few months after the attunement, I split up from my partner, which led me to run my new business venture in a foreign country on my own. My business is continuing to grow. I heal people on a physical, mental and spiritual program and so, I guess, I have really moved into my life's work or my soul path. This just continues to grow and I see life more and more from spirit."

Frances owns and runs a healing retreat named 'Gaia Visions' on the Greek island of Zakynthos. Before receiving Rupel's procedure, she had hoped to open this type of facility at some point in the future. In retrospect, it would appear that the procedure helped to make it a reality. Obviously, a crystal skull's ability to bring about change has also held true for Frances now that she can offer people healing and relaxation. During her recent trip to the UK, she purchased a small amethyst skull. It will be interesting to see how it impacts on Frances and her healing work.

In conclusion, I am happy to perform this DNA realignment/attunement procedure for anyone who feels the need to receive it. I make no charge for this service, but I do believe in an exchange of energies. Therefore, I always suggest that, if the recipients gain benefit from it, they send their thanks out to the Divine by doing a small, random act of kindness for another.

Chapter Five

THE TRAVELING SKULLS: PORTAL DE LUZ & MAHASAMATMAN

Two of the ancient crystal skulls, Max and Sha-Na-Ra, are often taken to lectures, workshops and seminars throughout America, as well as abroad. They help their custodians bring information about these amazing artifacts to the general public. They also give healing to anyone who comes into proximity with them. Max is a clear quartz skull, weighing approximately 18 lbs. It was a gift from the Guatemalan people to Norbu Chen, a Tibetan healer. Shortly before his death, he gave the skull to JoAnn and Carl Parks of Houston, Texas. Sha-Na-Ra was also carved from a clear quartz specimen that has a slight, yellowish tinge to it. This skull weighs approximately 13 lbs. and was discovered in Mexico by F. R. 'Nick' Nocerino in 1959.

Traveling around and working with groups of people

appears to be something that a number of contemporary crystal skulls are also doing. Molmec has displayed a preference for this and other crystal skull custodians have spoken of similar circumstances. In this chapter I am highlighting two such skulls.

Portal de Luz was fashioned from smoky quartz by a master carver in Minas Gerias, Brazil. This man has carved over one thousand skulls, and I believe he is the same person who carved Calenjo and Tol-Remy-Ran. Portal de Luz was a gift to Joshua "Illinois" Shapiro in May 1999 from his now ex-wife. He is close in size to the skull of an adult human and weighs approximately 10 lbs. Incidentally, I was fascinated to learn that Joshua has experienced the weight of his crystal skull increasing or decreasing when it is in a working mode. Portal de Luz has a flat, angular jaw and there is a great deal of detail in his facial features. Rainbows and colors have appeared within this skull when it is with people. Initially, there was some cloudiness throughout Portal de Luz, but this has lessened considerably.

Joshua is the co-founder of 'V J Enterprises,' which was officially formed in February 1992 and is located in the Chicago area. This company is dedicated to sharing the best available data on how our planet will be transformed into a Golden Age by the year 2013. The information is disseminated by means of an Internet website, lectures, workshops, interviews and the sale of relevant books. It includes details about crystal skulls, UFOs, Peru, Reiki, Healing, Networking and the New Age.

The first picture of a crystal skull that Joshua saw impacted strongly upon him. It was made from amethyst and was thought to be of ancient origin. This was in April of 1983 and although he had known about crystal skulls before this time, the image in the photograph seemed to trigger an awareness for him of working with crystal skulls in previous lifetimes. Since then, he has devoted his efforts into sharing with others his love of crystal skulls and his belief that they have a role to play within the future Golden Age. He has had the opportunity to visit and work with several of the ancient crystal skulls, including the Mitchell-Hedges Skull.

When Joshua is home, his crystal skull is kept either in his bedroom or in a special carrying bag, and it is often close by when he sleeps. He told me he does receive messages from the skull, but he cannot be certain whether they are actually coming from the skull or from spiritual beings who are using it as a means of communication. I was interested to hear that Joshua has a piece of rabbit fur on which he places Portal de Luz when he is giving lectures. Apparently, this skull requires a special setting. This is similar to Molmec's need for a cushion. Joshua added that a psychic friend has recently suggested using a silk scarf instead of the fur.

He described Portal de Luz's energy signature as "masculine," but he said this can become "feminine or androgynous" depending on with whom the skull is working. His observation agrees with my belief that a crystal skull changes its energy signature to suit a person's needs. Joshua believes that some of Portal de Luz's cloudiness has cleared as a consequence of the work they have done together. This includes "spiritual initiative consultations," being in the company of certain ancient crystal skulls and participating in the ceremonies of some indigenous people.

The skull travels with Joshua to various countries, where he presents workshops and lectures about crystal skulls. He also gives private consultations to those who are seeking spiritual healing and guidance. Within these sessions, people may request healing or ask questions about their spiritual development or other relevant matters. Joshua believes they do receive healing at some level and he also feels that with the help of his crystal skull, he is able to give them good counsel. Other people use the private session time to meditate with Portal de Luz. According to Joshua, his crystal skull "links into a person's energy and subtly sends what is important in that moment . . . " Portal de Luz also appears to have a very calming effect on people and helps them "open up to their spiritual gifts." Whether seeking answers or taking the opportunity for meditation, participants in these sessions have reported seeing scenes within the skull or have felt an extremely strong energy coming from it. Others have experienced profound visions.

Joshua told me that certain individuals, who are known to him as Star People and Wanderers, seem to be particularly drawn to his crystal skull. When I asked him for an explanation of these names, he told me they are "ET souls that have incarnated into the earth to help with the transformation of the Golden Age." Wanderers is an expression with which I am familiar. In April 1993 my angelic guides first told me about Wanderers within a channeled reading that I was conducting for someone. They explained that Wanderers are souls who do not always reincarnate into the same universe. They wander from one universe to another, living one lifetime in one universe, but then moving to a different universe for the next life. Whereas, the souls, who are not Wanderers, live all of their incarnations in the same universe. My guides also told me there are many Wanderers living on our planet at this time because they want to observe and participate in the coming Earth Changes.

I asked Joshua if he believed Portal de Luz had come into his life at a time of change or whether this skull had initiated change for him. He answered that the latter was true, saying, "It initiated a life change in that I learned how to become a true crystal skull caretaker." I also questioned him if, initially, he had any feelings of fear or apprehension about crystal skulls. His response, I feel, is very insightful:

> "I have never been afraid of the crystal skulls. I know deep within me that their true purpose is to be a spiritual tool to awaken the divinity within us. The

image of a skull has been used by the dark side to frighten people from working with the skulls in the past. How can we be afraid of something that is a part of our body? Are we saying our skulls are evil?"

Joshua is the author of several books on UFOs and the Aquarian Age. Within his travels and research work into crystal skulls, he has found many leads and connections to UFO experiences. He is also the co-author, together with Sandra Bowen and F. R. Nocerino, of the book *Mysteries of the Crystal Skulls Revealed*, which was published in 1989. At the present time, he is writing his next book that has the working title *Journeys of a Crystal Skull Explorer*. It will include stories about his travels and experiences with some of the ancient crystal skulls, together with information on certain "incredible people" he has met. Other subjects covered will be Joshua's personal search in South America for a blue crystal skull, and the scientific and paranormal research that is being done in order to understand how a crystal skull functions.

During his most recent trip to Europe, Joshua stayed in my home for several days. This gave me the opportunity to become acquainted with Portal de Luz. I put this crystal skull on the coffee table in my living room, which is the same room that houses my collection of skulls. At Joshua's suggestion and on different days, I positioned several of my crystal skulls close to Portal de Luz so that there could be an exchange of energy between them. All of the skulls, including Joshua's, seemed to benefit from this action. Rainbow irising appeared within all of them during these times. I also placed Portal de Luz on my bedside table one night and was awakened at one point with the strong impression that the skull had asked me to place my hand on him. I did this and quickly drifted back into sleep. On waking in the morning, I was surprised to find my hand was covering the skull's face. This was the exact position where I had placed it hours before.

My first impression of Portal de Luz was that he is a serious and hard working, spiritual tool. It also felt very obvious to me that he has been in the company of several of the ancient crystal skulls. There was an air of solemnity and a true spiritual vibration coming from him. Before leaving my home, I believe, this skull thanked me for his mini vacation and he seemed to be recharged and ready for his esoteric work in Belgium, Holland and Germany.

Within his busy schedule, Joshua is also working to create two research centers, one in the US and the other in the UK. Eventually, he hopes to establish further centers in Brazil and Australia. His aim for these places is to share through classes, workshops and local networking, new information and insights into various world mysteries, including crystal skulls and UFOs. In addition, he foresees these centers as becoming places of sanctuary for some of the world's crystal skulls.

* * *

Kathleen Murray lives in the North-East of Scotland in a small village named Rhynie, which is about thirty-eight miles west of Aberdeen. There are fifty-nine stone circles throughout Aberdeenshire and, through guidance, she has also constructed a stone circle in her backyard. This worthy project has been dedicated by Kathleen to the devic kingdom. One of these standing stones is a 644 kilo block of rose quartz, an earth keeper, that came from Brazil and is called Divineva. This huge mineral specimen was shipped to Scotland in time for the Summer Solstice of 1996.

Prior to the arrival of her first crystal skull, Kathleen had been involved in working with several crystal spheres. As a point of interest, I believe there is a strong connection between spheres and skulls that have been carved from minerals. My research has shown that a number of people, who are initially attracted to working with crystal spheres, gravitate eventually towards the crystal skulls. Scrying is possible with both spheres and skulls, but I think there is a deeper connection between these two forms.

Within what Kathleen refers to as her "earthworking," which is a form of planetary healing made possible with the help of the devic kingdom, she was guided to ask for assistance. This was in 1996. She presumed this aid would be given in the form of a person, who would arrive in order to help her with her work. Soon after making the request, she learned from an acquaintance, who imports mineral specimens from Brazil, that he had a crystal skull, which might interest her. The skull had been ordered for a customer, but this person had changed his mind after the skull was shipped. As soon as the skull arrived, Kathleen became aware that it was communicating with her. It was obvious that it had come in answer to her request for help. Sometime afterwards, this crystal skull was an important part of activation ceremonies conducted by Kathleen for three mandalas and a stone circle.

In time, the skull gave her its name as Mahasamatman and that its energy vibration was projective. However, at a later date, on the arrival of another crystal skull, it changed to receptive. Again, this would corroborate my findings with regards the energy signature of crystal skulls. Mahasamatman was fashioned from clear quartz and weighs approximately 5 lbs. Kathleen describes her crystal skull as having:

> "... veils and a shield/plane towards the back of his skull ... He/she has very fine features, like a well groomed gentleman/lady. His teeth look hand carved, as does the interesting shape in his nose space. He/she is not symmetrical and, if looked at closely, is squint!"

Mahasamatman told Kathleen that he was "created in light and then manifest on the earth plane through a vortex in Brazil ... " Two months after the skull's arrival, she had the opportunity to travel to Brazil with the hope of tracking down Mahasamatman's origin. She visited the company, which produces many of the contemporary crystal skulls that come from Brazil. The people she contacted did not recognize Mahasamatman as being the work of one of their master carvers. They said they could not carve one like him and that they use a different technique. This information, together with her other experiences with Mahasamatman, has convinced Kathleen that this crystal skull was fashioned somewhere other than our planet.

During her visit to Brazil in the summer of 1996, Kathleen visited some caves. When she set Mahasamatman down on the floor of a large cavern, she observed twelve etheric skulls forming a circle around him. Beams of light radiated from the skulls to Mahasamatman and also back from him to them. This effect formed a twelve-pointed star of many colors. She later learned that each of these skulls is connected to a galaxy or star system within our universe, and transmits messages from some universal intelligences. Kathleen now channels the words of these beings.

In October 1996, she revisited Brazil. One day, while there, she felt drawn to look into the base of her crystal skull, and she became aware of the presence of certain beings. Kathleen also felt compelled to write their words and was told that they could be known as the Galactic Masters. They explained that, together with Mahasamatman, they form the Team of Thirteen that seeded humanity. Apparently, these beings are making their presence known to us at this time in order to help with our progression.

Kathleen's adventures with Mahasamatman in Brazil, her linking to specific sites and vortices there, together with her channelings, are detailed in her book *The Divine Spark of Creation: The Crystal Skull Speaks*. This narrative is available in a boxed set with thirteen separate skull photographs, each one in a different color. These pictures can be used as meditation tools or in any other way that feels appropriate.

There is a meditation room in Kathleen's home that has many crystals in it. Mahasamatman usually stays in this room, when he is not traveling with her. Depending on with whom he is working, he prefers to be placed on material of certain colors. Like Molmec, his cloth-of-choice is velvet. Kathleen sees Mahasamatman as "a healing skull with universal healing information, and lots of stories to tell." She added, "When he is out with people, I see him healing them without any need for language." Kathleen gives workshops with Mahasamatman in various places in the UK, including Glastonbury.

I asked Kathleen if she ever takes her crystal skull to bed with her and if he had appeared in any of her dreams. She answered:

> "At times, when I ask for personal help, he sleeps with me. He does appear in dreams to me and to people around the world, sometimes before they have met him."

I also questioned Kathleen about whether Mahasamatman came into her life at a time of change. As with other crystal skull custodians, her reply emphasizes the close connection between these mineral carvings and transformation: "Yes, and the changes since have been colossal, and are ongoing." She added, "He is a major accelerator on my journey."

In answer to my question about whether she had felt any apprehension in the beginning towards working with a skull, she replied:

> "I have had my own fears to overcome, and I am interested in tracking the roots of these fears, which, I believe, are forms of control inserted into our subconscious in other lifetimes."

There is more information about Kathleen Murray and her other two crystal skulls in the following chapter.

Chapter Six

OTHER CRYSTAL SKULL CUSTODIANS

Mark Loman lives in the town of Yeovil in Somerset, England. He describes himself as "a jewel doctor," being an accomplished goldsmith who creates beautiful pieces of jewelry and repairs antique gemstone items. He has worked for a number of years with the mineral kingdom, both in his professional capacity and as an admirer of gems and crystals. He is also an Elestial Reiki Master, a Tarot card reader and a man who is pursuing his spiritual progression.

I first heard about Mark in September 2000 from Sam Elliott. I had met Sam the previous year, when I attuned her to the mastership level of Elestial Reiki. This is a form of 'hands-on' healing that I developed in 1997. It is a blending of Traditional Usui Reiki with Essential Reiki, which was created by Diane Stein, and it is combined with the power of the mineral kingdom. Sam informed me that she would be attuning two of her students to the mastership level during

October 2000. She thought I might be interested in making contact with one of them, namely Mark, because, like me, he held a passion for crystal skulls. Soon afterwards, Mark and I established a relationship through emails and, eventually, he visited me. Since then, a strong friendship has grown up between us.

The first time Mark saw a crystal skull was in September 1998 at the Mind Body Spirit Festival in London. It impacted on him quite strongly. He wanted to buy it, but felt the price was too expensive. About a year later, a friend told Mark that she was reading a fascinating book entitled *The Mystery of the Crystal Skulls*. She recommended that he read it. He recalled the crystal skull he had seen previously at the Festival and felt that he was being guided towards these crystal carvings. As if to verify this feeling, he saw a small skull pendant that was fashioned from phantom quartz in a shop in Yeovil. Phantom crystals are considered very special within esoteric circles. In my own experience, they have proved to be an excellent tool for past life regression. The scientific explanation for them is that they are a crystal that grew, then stopped, but began growing, again. This has created a crystal within a crystal. Sometimes this process occurred over and over and the outlines of earlier crystal formations are clearly visible within the ultimate crystal. Mark purchased the pendant and that began his fascination with these mineral carvings. To date, he has over eighty crystal skulls of varying sizes in his keeping, the largest one being Wenjo, a beautiful, 15 lb. African jasper skull. These mineral friends have initiated change for Mark, guiding him into taking a keen interest in Reiki, Crystal Therapy and shamanic drumming.

As each new skull arrives at his home, Mark cleanses it and then gives it the Elestial Reiki attunements. This is a unique approach to caring for mineral specimens. With regards this interesting practice, Mark said, "The skulls really like being attuned to Reiki, they glitter like mad afterwards, and

I find I don't have to cleanse them as they do it for themselves . . . " As a point of interest, I gave Cheiron the Elestial Reiki first level attunement a while after I purchased this skull. It was soon after this that I noticed many of the cranium indentations had disappeared.

Mark's crystal skulls are all housed in his living room. At least half of them sit on a table, while others are in a glass case, or on top of the TV, or dotted around the room. One of these skulls, named Morgan, is always with him when he is out and about. Carved from labradorite and displaying a receptive energy signature, Morgan is similar in size to Lopa, but was carved in a totally different style. She also appears to be inseparable from Mark. He describes her as "a naughty child" who demands to be taken everywhere he is going, including to work, to visit friends and on shopping sprees. When he is buying new crystal skulls, she either encourages him to buy a particular one or tells him she does not like certain other ones.

I questioned Mark about how he receives messages from Morgan and he said he can definitely hear her talking to him. If he ignores her requests to be taken to places with him, he said, "she positively screams" at him. He usually carries her in a pocket or in a tote bag. While driving past Stonehenge on several different days, Morgan has told him she wants to go there, but he is waiting for one of those few occasions when it is open to the public.

When Morgan first came to live with Mark, he took her into bed with him on most nights, but rarely does this now. Sleeping with a new crystal skull is normal practice for him, and I have also found this to be true for both me and my husband. Perhaps this is necessary to establish a close bond with a new addition to our crystal skull collections? It seems feasible to me that a skull could build a link for communication and friendship more easily while its custodian sleeps. The conscious state or "beta brain wave pattern" is not naturally conducive to metaphysical work. For many of us it takes time and discipline to consciously accept the esoteric side of life.

Two other skulls help Mark with his Elestial Reiki work. They are Shadow, a 3 lb. clear quartz/chlorite phantom specimen, and Hope, who was carved from rainbow obsidian and weighs 3.50 lbs. Shadow presents a projective energy vibration and Hope displays a receptive one. When giving Reiki healing to a client, Mark places Shadow in line with the crown chakra and puts Hope close to the base/root chakra. By placing crystals within the vicinity of the crown and base chakras, a connection is formed between the two. This ensures an appropriate balance of the spiritual persona with the physical ego during healing or any other metaphysical act. Obsidian helps us with our connection to the Earth Mother, it is a grounding crystal. Therefore, placing it on or near the base chakra also 'earths' or brings into physical reality the benefit of any healing that may be taking place at another level. Mark described the actions of these two crystal skulls during a healing session as follows: "Shadow is winkling out any hidden baggage, bringing it out to be dealt with, while Hope helps to earth it." He said that one of his clients cried "so hard and so deeply" while receiving Reiki healing with these two skulls. She told him she felt "a great weight" had been taken away and that she had cleared about twenty years of problems and negativity.

Milo is a third skull that assists Mark within the use of Reiki. Fashioned from clear quartz into a grape-size skull, he gives a projective energy signature. A few months ago, Mark was directed by Milo to set him into a ring consisting of 22 ct. gold and silver. This is now a stunning piece of jewelry. When giving Elestial Reiki attunements, Mark uses Hope as a grounding tool for the procedure and Milo is either in his hand or on one of his fingers, when he traces the Reiki symbols.

Another clear quartz skull, named Denuvian, came into Mark's keeping in early May of 2001. This skull was created by the same Brazilian master carver who sculpted Portal de

Luz. Denuvian weighs 3 lbs. and presents a projective vibration. Within his internal structure, there is a facet that mimics a flaw running vertically through the middle of this skull. When viewed from one side, this structure resembles a rippling waterfall. The opposite side of this facet displays many beautiful rainbows.

Denuvian, in my opinion, is a very special crystal skull and there is more information about him in Chapter Seven. At the time of writing, he is on loan for six months to a friend of a friend of Mark's. This woman is extremely psychic and clairvoyant and has recently been receiving messages from a spirit guide named Lightning. According to this being, he comes from a blue universe and has requested the assistance of Denuvian. With the skull's help, the woman will be able to channel information on something named "blue ray healing." I am eagerly awaiting feedback on this situation.

As a point of interest, Mark also has become aware that his crystal skulls adjust their positions from time to time. We discussed this matter, and his experience of this occurrence is very similar to mine.

In August 2001, he and I gave a workshop on contemporary crystal skulls at the previously mentioned Festival of Holistic Living in London. This event was very well attended and was received with enthusiasm and applause. I have experienced similar responses previously, when I have conducted workshops on the ancient crystal skulls. I believe this demonstrates the curiosity and keen interest that a growing number of people have about these mineral carvings. During our workshop, each participant was able to work one-on-one with a crystal skull and also to receive healing from it. At the end of the workshop, the majority of the people were very reluctant to give back their new crystal friends. It was obvious that a strong connection had been created between them.

Immediately after the Festival, a woman, named Sue Bouvier from Kent in England, emailed Mark. Sue was a participant in our workshop and had meditated with Denuvian. She wanted to give Mark feedback on what she had experienced. Apparently, the skull had vibrated while she held it, and had shown her the symbol of a pyramid. She also felt the energy vibration of this skull was receptive, which was the opposite to what Mark had been given. I think this is one more example of a crystal skull presenting itself differently to separate people. Mark had also been shown pyramids by Denuvian in an earlier meditation and there are further details about these structures in Chapter Seven. Since attending the workshop, Sue has quickly become friends with Mark.

※ ※ ※

It is only within the past couple of years that Sue Bouvier has become interested in the mineral kingdom. She was directed towards Crystal Therapy by a friend, whom she had met at the National Federation of Spiritual Healers (NFSH). This friend also helped her realize how 'in tune' she really was to Druidry and Paganism. Previously, Sue had been unaware of her affinity with these spiritual pursuits. At the present time, she is taking training to become a qualified crystal healing practitioner.

The first crystal skulls that Sue encountered were at the same friend's home, and her reaction to them was to say that they were "macabre." Her initial interaction with a crystal skull was during her first year of crystal healing training. There were many different types of crystals at the training college, which students could work with or even buy and, on one occasion, Sue felt drawn towards a small skull carved from clear quartz. Not liking skulls, she picked it up and put it back down several times, but, finally, felt compelled to work with the skull. As she explained:

"I had to pick it up, but didn't understand how I could pick up and work with something I didn't

> like . . . I had the feeling that this skull had, in fact, chosen me and that in doing so it had its reasons."

On that particular day the students learned how to cleanse and dedicate crystals and, while doing these procedures, Sue experienced the skull vibrating in her hand. Further visits to her friend's home did nothing to change her opinion of crystal skulls, but after reading *The Mystery of the Crystal Skulls*, which the friend let her borrow, Sue could accept that the ancient crystal skulls had unusual properties. However, she felt there was no connection between them and their contemporary counterparts.

Several months later, Sue went to the August Festival of Holistic Living and attended the workshop that Mark and I gave. This event obviously impacted upon her and appears to have helped change her feelings towards the image of a skull. When I interviewed Sue, she told me she felt the workshop had "opened up something inside" her. She added:

> "The skull (Denuvian) had a profound effect on me. As I sat down and looked at the skulls on the table, I found myself being drawn to one in particular. We were told we would be meditating with them . . . When it came to my turn, I asked for that skull. I had an immediate affinity with it."

During the first meditation, Sue saw the pyramid and felt the skull vibrate. When she meditated with Denuvian a second time, she saw "an Egyptian princess with black hair and dressed in turquoise." She also heard "Tibetan cymbals, which had a very clear, feminine ring to them." The woman within the vision told Sue she would be moving forward into channeling, and the tool that would help her with this would be a crystal skull. In addition, she said Sue was not yet ready to begin this work, but that when she was, the right crystal skull would find her.

Several weeks after attending the workshop, Sue had a second encounter with the small skull at the training college. Within a practical healing exercise, the tutor exchanged one of the crystals chosen by the two students who were giving Sue healing. The crystal had been placed near Sue's crown chakra and the tutor removed it and put the clear quartz skull in its place. Afterwards, she could not understand why she had done this, she did not usually interfere with her students' choices of crystals. She could only state that she was being "screamed at" to use the skull. When the healing session was over, Sue was surprised to learn that the skull had taken part in the healing. She held it for a few moments and knew that his name was Freddie.

On the train journey going home that day, Sue repeatedly saw an image of the little skull in front of her. Then she saw a Premium Bond check for £50, which was the exact cost of the skull. In the UK people purchase Premium Bonds as a way of saving money. Each Bond has its own number and these numbers are regularly placed in a drawing for monetary wins. Both images were so insistent that Sue made a promise to herself—if she was fortunate enough to receive such a check that month, she would only spend the money on the skull. As she said, "Something told me that if I used this money for anything else, it would rebound on me." When she arrived home, that day's mail was waiting for her and one envelope contained a Premium Bond check for £50. Her vision had come true, she had won the money with which to buy the skull. Sue purchased Freddie and he has become her close companion. I also believe he is the skull referred to within her second meditation with Denuvian because Sue is now a voice channel.

Knowing that Sue's opinion about crystal skulls had changed, her friend sent Sue a fluorite skull for her birthday. This one is named Karr and is to help with earth healing. Freddie and Karr have been impacting on her dreams and, I am sure, have helped Sue become yet another person who is enchanted with crystal skulls. Her words reflect what happens to all who take them into their keeping: "I have changed my perception of skulls completely now."

* * *

I have known Linda, who lives in London, England, for more than six years. She is a good friend who prefers, within this book, to just be known by her first name. I originally met her when she attended one of my workshops on crystals. Since that time, she has taken training in several other metaphysical subjects, including Crystal Therapy, Qi Gong, Elestial Reiki, Native American Spirituality and Spiritual Development. She is also a reflexologist.

In October 1999, while visiting me at my home, Linda purchased one of our Brazilian crystal skulls. She had previously seen our skull collection during other visits. She had felt their power and was sure a person could accomplish a great deal with their help. However, she was somewhat wary of them. On this particular occasion, we had recently received several new skulls and Linda was immediately drawn to one of them. She picked it up and held it throughout the extent of her visit. When it was time for her to leave, she could not go without her new friend.

Prior to Linda seeing this crystal skull, I had already spent some time holding it and receiving impressions from it. I was given its name as being Femrii and that it has a receptive energy vibration. This skull appeared to be a powerful metaphysical tool that is not for the faint-hearted. Femrii can connect those who work with her to the archetypal energy of the fire goddesses, e.g. Pele, Kali, Copper Woman, Tonantzin, etc. She is the same size as Tol-Remy-Ran and was carved from smoky quartz. There is some rainbow irising within her depths and some fleck inclusions of an orange/brown mineral, possibly carnelian, in the base of the cranium. I have seen Femrii a number of times since she left my home and these flecks appear to be increasing. She has also gained more clarity, and the depth of her color has lightened.

Linda describes her crystal skull as "a fireball, no nonsense" individual. When she first brought Femrii home, Linda was not sure whether she was ready to work with her. She put her in her spare room and kept her close to a piece of rose quartz. This seemed to tone down the skull's fiery nature. While holding Femrii, Linda felt this crystal skull was connecting with her brain and brow chakra. She believes Femrii can promote the development of the third eye, but she has not felt ready to pursue this as yet. Linda also thinks this skull is not a healer, but teaches "respect for the elemental forces."

In later months, Linda moved Femrii to her bedroom. She placed her on a window-sill, but recently has thought about moving this skull closer to her bed. Linda is careful about whom she allows to handle Femrii because she is aware how powerful this mineral carving is. As she explained, "It all depends on how you interact with that power."

Femrii certainly came into Linda's life at a time of great change. She had just begun a new job and was also dealing with the upset of learning that her father was very ill with cancer. Looking back, she says, "It was a time of turmoil" and that she was "only just able to hold things together." She believes Femrii helped her to be strong and also "get in touch" with herself. Linda does, however, feel that this crystal skull had to "soften a bit" so that they could have a better understanding of each other. Her early impression of Femrii was one of seriousness, but now she seems less intense.

When I asked Linda what else she thought Femrii has done for her, she explained that this skull has given her support, has made her "more finely tuned on the subtle level" and has "kept open a window of opportunity" for her. Also, since becoming Femrii's custodian, Linda has developed an interest in the Tarot and has gained the second level of Elestial Reiki. She added that she really loves her crystal skull. To date, Femrii has not shared with Linda any other name by which she can know her.

Since Femrii came to stay with Linda, she has given her the impression that she did not want the company of other crystal skulls. However, several weeks ago, Linda felt prompted to buy a plum-size, rose quartz skull. When she asked for the name of the skull, she was told "Magi." Remembering that this was the name of the three wise men, Linda remarked that she thought there were three of them. To this the skull replied, "I am three." When Linda gave me this information by email, it was like déjà-vu for me. Several days before, Mark Loman had told me that as he unpacked a new addition to his collection, a large amethyst skull, it had given its name as Magi. We are now waiting to hear of a third crystal skull with the same name.

At first, Linda was apprehensive about how Femrii would receive Magi because, as she says, "They couldn't be more different." However, they are both positioned on her bedroom window-sill and appear to be working well together. Linda describes Magi as "incredibly positive and constructive" and that this crystal skull is "utilizing and seeking to resolve all the big things that Femrii brings up."

* * *

Paula, another close friend, who also lives in London and chooses anonymity, purchased two grape-size crystal skulls in 1999. Their origin is unknown, but they were obtained from a retail company in the US that sells crystals and mineral carvings. This friend felt drawn to the skulls, but, like Linda, was somewhat unsure of them. She has been a loving collector of crystals for many years and was aware of the power within crystal skulls. One skull, named Zenir, is clear quartz with a chlorite inclusion in the cranium, and the other, Xuana, was carved from rose quartz. She reports that the clarity of Zenir has improved since coming to her and the green color of the chlorite has intensified. Zenir displays a projective energy vibration and Xuana's is receptive.

Paula placed these skulls together in her bedroom, but did not always feel comfortable with their presence in there. She also tried having them in her living room and moved them back and forth for some time. Eventually, after many months, she brought them into her living room, where they have remained. She believes they told her, "Yes, this is the spot. We will reside here." Paula explained, "It now feels happier and lighter with them there."

In response to my question about how she feels the two skulls have impacted upon her, she told me that Zenir always appears to be pushing her into doing the things about which she sometimes procrastinates. Whereas, Xuana is much more gentle in her approach and seems to be easing and soothing Zenir's urgency. This would appear to be a similar effect to that which the rose quartz specimen had on Femrii. Paula added that whenever there is "turbulent energy" in the building where she lives, caused by such things as neighbors quarreling, her attention seems to be drawn to Zenir. At these times, the skull "appears more opaque/cloudy." She feels Zenir is acting like a warning system by showing her a less-than-clear appearance.

With regards any changes the skulls may have brought into her life, Paula believes they prompted her to "not just feel compassion, but to manifest it in a physical, practical and, hopefully, helpful way." Since their arrival, she has decided to compile a dictionary of herbs and medicinal plants. This has been a time-consuming and difficult task as the appropriate names are given in several different languages. It has also been a labor of love because she plans to donate all of the proceeds from the sale of this book to The Land Mine Appeal. At the time of writing, this laudable project is nearing completion.

In April 2001, I gave Paula an egg-size, Chinese fluorite skull for her birthday. Although, as yet, she has not been given a name for this skull, she believes its energy signature is receptive. Paula also feels very closely bonded with it. She keeps this skull on a shelf next to her bed, together with several other crystals. When she lays back to read or to go to sleep, she either places the skull on her chest or holds it in the palm of her hand. This fluorite skull has become a dear companion from whom she would not want to be parted.

* * *

C. 'Ravenia' Todd is a Canadian woman from British Columbia who owns an online, retail business that sells contemporary crystal skulls. She pursues a number of metaphysical interests, including Spiritualism, Astrology, Numerology, Aromatherapy and all aspects of psychic phenomenon. Ravenia is also interested in the Runes and various other forms of divination, together with telepathic communication with animals.

She became interested in these mineral carvings about four years ago, when she purchased her first crystal skull. This happened soon after she had seen a black skull during a dream. There is further information about Ravenia's dream in Chapter Seven. The skull she bought was carved from snowflake obsidian, weighs 7.22 lbs. and displays a receptive energy signature. She is close to being life-size. In order to cleanse her new friend, Ravenia buried her in the earth for one lunar month. She related what happened then:

"When I unearthed her, the name Belinda kept bombarding my mind. I had consciously decided earlier that I would name the skull Raven. I have had a life-long admiration/fascination for the corvid family. As well, the seller of the skull had told me that the man, who carved the skull, is named Raven. However, the name Belinda persisted, so I relented and called this obsidian skull Belinda."

Apparently, Belinda came into Ravenia's life at a time of change. Her words echo my own and others' findings about crystal skulls:

> "Belinda taught me that skulls tend to be about change. She arrived just before unforeseen changes began occurring in my life . . . Through an unusual series of events shortly after I got Belinda, I came in contact with Raven, Belinda's creator. He is a master carver and the owner/manager of 'Raven's Roost,' which is the oldest, largest, and finest crystal skull company in the world.
>
> I purchased a few more skulls over the course of several months. I became quite mesmerized with these carvings and realized that they 'put' me into a different space when I was in their presence . . . I had my first scrying experience with a smoky/citrine/clear quartz skull, and I believe it was at that point that I knew I was hooked!
>
> Meanwhile, Raven and I became good friends through emails and, eventually, phone calls. We were both amazed at the similarities in our lives. Within the year, I had met Raven in person and the rest is history. He and I have much in common and in short order we were head-over-heels in love and remain that way to this day. I feel Belinda was a catalyst for the beginnings of this relationship . . ."

When speaking further about Raven Youngman, she said:

"He is the person solely responsible for the refinements in crystal skull carvings over the past couple of decades. The hollowed jaws/cheeks/nasal passages features are completely his creations. He has been creating skulls for over 25 years and is very highly respected in the lapidary world. He holds the largest inventory of crystal/gemstone skulls worldwide with more than 8,000 skulls in the shop and more in production at any given time. Raven truly is The Skullmaster of this age!

Now, a few years after Belinda's arrival, my life has completely changed. I have a wonderful relationship with a kind, intelligent, special man. As well, I am in an entirely different line of work, which revolves specifically around crystal skulls. I have developed my own retail business, 'Thought and Memory,' which has me dealing with the skulls on a full time basis. I also assist Raven with 'Raven's Roost,' whenever needed. I feel that I was specifically guided to meet Raven and become involved with the skulls. I feel privileged to assist these wonderful healing tools of Light find their way to their intended keepers around the globe. Every time a skull goes out to its new owner, I feel that I have performed a service for the planetary, crystalline grid."

In answer to my questions about where Ravenia keeps her snowflake obsidian skull, she said, "Belinda resides in my bedroom, along with 75-80 other skulls. It's starting to get crowded!"

Another of Ravenia's crystal skulls is named Atsiitsiin. Carved from black tourmaline with a green tourmaline inclusion, he presents a projective energy signature and weighs 3.61 lbs. Like Portal de Luz and Mahasamatman, Atsiitsiin appears to enjoy traveling. Ravenia explained:

> "This skull has done some traveling, including touring across the American Southwest. I have taken Atsiitsiin to the Navajo Reservation in North-East Arizona. There we experienced the ancient energy of Canyon de Chelly and Canyon del Muerto, where the mysterious Anasazi people built their cliff dwellings. It was in Canyon del Muerto that Atsiitsiin received his name. Atsiitsiin is the Navajo word for skull."

Ravenia photographed her tourmaline skull while visiting the Anasazi Cliff Dwellings in Canyon del Muerto. The photograph forms part of the front cover of this book.

Atsiitsiin has also accompanied Ravenia when she visited several ancient and sacred sites within the US, including the Garden of the Gods and the Cave of the Winds, both of which are near Manitou Springs in Colorado. While inside the Cave of the Winds with Atsiitsiin, Ravenia took some photographs that proved to be very interesting. She said:

> "... I photographed many anomalies that my eye couldn't see, but the camera picked up anyway. Interestingly enough, I photographed very similar looking anomalies in the Grand Canyon Caverns a month later. Atsiitsiin was also in attendance at the Grand Canyon Caverns. However, he wasn't with me when I went through Colossal Cave near Tucson, Arizona, and no anomalies showed up in my photos from that particular cave. The same camera was used in each cave."

Ravenia forwarded the above mentioned photographs to me via email. The anomalies she spoke of are small spheres of light that appear to be floating within the image taken and in front of the camera lens. I am familiar with these anomalies because they have appeared on photographs taken with digital cameras by other people. It is thought that this type of camera can pick up unseen phenomena. There was some research done recently in the UK in which digital photographs were taken while inside a building that is known to be haunted. Similar spheres were evident in the photographs. They were nebulous and two-dimensional. It is possible that they are a representation of spirits. The spheres in Ravenia's photographs appear more solid and somewhat three-dimensional. I believe the presence of Atsiitsiin helped to bring them into better focus.

This crystal skull has been fortunate enough to also experience the vortex energy that exists at Bell Rock, Red Rock Crossing and Cathedral Rock in Sedona, Arizona. While in Sedona, Ravenia had an aura photograph taken of herself with Atsiitsiin. Apparently, this was something of interest to the photographer. Ravenia told me:

> "The photographer was intrigued with my request, she had not photographed stones before. She was quite amazed when the photo showed a broad, dark indigo aura around the skull!"

The third crystal skull that Ravenia feels very close to is a larger than life-size, Russian clear quartz specimen. Named Perkins, he weighs in at a hefty 21.84 lbs. This skull displays a projective energy vibration and is the largest carving in her ever-growing crystal skull collection. Ravenia has had some interesting experiences with Perkins:

> "This is a truly amazing skull that I am extremely fond of. Often there are remarkable images inside the crystal cranium. These images seem to have a life all

of their own. There are two faces that I have seen often, I refer to them as Jack and Jill. I have also seen skulls inside Perkins..."

In order to elaborate on what sometimes appears inside the skull, she sent me a photograph of Perkins with an arrow pointing to the image of a small skull within his cranium. She added, "... this is very typical of this big skull, he is a very visual skull."

The fact that Ravenia has observed these things inside Perkins is not surprising. People, who have been fortunate enough to spend time with the Mitchell-Hedges Skull, also report seeing scenes and images that come and go. Some appear to be reflections of ancient civilizations, while others are of alien landscapes. Apparently, skulls fashioned from clear quartz have the ability to display other times and dimensions to us. Ravenia has her own theory about what Perkins has shown:

"Judging by the expressions that appear, there are times that Perkins appears very excitable, and other times that the mood expressed is more laid-back and relaxed. Raven has also experienced this imaging phenomenon with Perkins on several occasions. I sense that these faces are reflections of discarnate entities, who are using Perkins as a 'looking glass' to see our physical world through."

As with Atsiitsiin, Ravenia has had an aura photograph taken of herself with Perkins. She told me:

"Recently, I took Perkins to an aura photographer. We took two aura photos—the first one of me with the skull completely removed from the room and the second one immediately after with the skull on my lap. The resulting photos are quite remarkable! The first photo shows predominantly lower chakra colors, lots of unorganized, mental activity, etc. The second photo with Perkins on my lap shows all upper chakra colors in my aura, definitely a more spiritual energy around me. Also, two individual entities appeared in front of me, one is masculine and one is feminine. I intuitively feel that these two entities are associated specifically/constantly with Perkins, perhaps being Jack and Jill."

I asked Ravenia if she had noticed whether her crystal skulls appeared to slightly move their positions at times. She said she had not experienced this, but was aware that it could happen. Several other skull custodians had informed her that they were encountering this phenomenon.

Ravenia believes there is a growing interest in crystal skulls. Within the past year, she has sold far more of them than in previous years. She added that many of the crystal skulls in her stock are being bought by people in the United Kingdom. Ravenia theorizes that the skulls are needed by people as a way of helping them "cope with the various stresses and changes in our world that affect us all to some degree." She also said:

"The earth is in a period of transition and, since humans tend to fear the unknown and change in general, it seems the skulls are really needed here at this time. I truly believe that is why there seems to be a growing interest and demand for them."

Summing up her feelings about crystal skulls, Ravenia told me, "I feel honored to be associated with the skulls on the level that I am." For her, living with them is both "interesting and rewarding." She has had many unusual experiences with her crystals skulls and hopes to write a book about them one day.

* * *

In September 2000, Kathleen Murray's second crystal skull came to live with her. He was carved from smoky quartz in, she believes, China. This is a life-size skull, weighing 13 lbs. and having a projective vibration. A very close friend of Kathleen's was given the name Kalif for this contemporary skull. True to a crystal skull's ability to bring about change, Kalif's arrival heralded the news that the close friend and the father of Kathleen's newborn daughter, were both suffering from cancer. As Kathleen explained:

> "So my two most intimate relationships in my life had cancer! I had to find ways of helping with healing in depths, to help them and help myself cope with anger, pain, grief, vulnerability, and loss . . . I was barely able to function, to mother my two girls during the day and process my emotions during the night. So I asked for help."

When we ask for this type of help, particularly if the request is made of the mineral kingdom, it is always given. For Kathleen the support came from 'Crystal Keys—The Wholeness of Lemurian Wisdom,' which she says, "was birthed through Kalif." This is a vibrational healing modality that encompasses crystals, sound, color, symbols and remedies. Through channeling, Kathleen was given twenty-two symbols and fourteen 'Imprints of Wholeness in Light.' She added that the latter "balance all our emotional, mental, physical and spiritual bodies."

Soon afterwards, a developing awareness of 'Crystal Keys' allowed her to accept the loss of her close friend, who succumbed to the cancer. However, Kathleen believes their friendship continues, even after death. She said:

> "She has helped me greatly from the other side to bring my Crystal Keys teaching through. The channeling of this healing system only fully came through after her death, and so her soul's journey with mine continues . . . I do mourn my loss of her companionship, at times, and, at other times, I am so grateful for all I have received."

Kathleen now teaches this healing process through workshops and an Internet website. She told me:

> "When I teach this now, I have painted the orbs of golden light into a set of 14 Imprints of Wholeness . . . I have drawn the 22 symbols, so people can use dowsing to find the roots of the problem to be healed. This is a very powerful healing wisdom and I really enjoy sharing this. So many people need help at this time to heal themselves and others, especially with cancer and other life-threatening diseases."

About a year after Kalif's arrival, in September 2001, another crystal skull came into Kathleen's keeping. This is Jade, a hollowed out, life-size skull that weighs 11 lbs. Carved from the mineral jade and displaying a receptive energy signature, she is thought to be of ancient origin. Kathleen also shared the following information about Jade:

> " . . . I was offered to be the guardian of an ancient, jade skull, found in a tomb in Mongolia. Jade, as I have called her now, has sigils/symbols from the unconscious carved on top of her skull, with a stamp of hieroglyphic writing on the base . . . researchers

think she could be from 2,500-6,000 years old, though no one really knows. Since she was handed into my care, she has lost the white, crusty look she had, and the jade has come to life with many different colors through an overall green."

As with Kalif, this skull came to Kathleen when she was experiencing difficulties within her personal life, and these, in turn, were affecting her hours of sleep. However, becoming Jade's custodian has definitely alleviated this problem for Kathleen. She explained:

"... And to have Jade join me, as she did, when I was handling some very challenging healing of my heart and soul, seemed to me to be a gift from the universe. One of the valuable things she did was to help retrain my sleep patterns (of course, easy for her as she works from the unconscious mind)."

Today, Kathleen is busy raising her two daughters and teaching others about crystal skulls, earth healing and the devic kingdom. She expresses the difficulties she has overcome as "human hell and multiple crises," but she believes her "inner spirit soared and grew." She also attributes her conquest of these difficulties to the support that has come from other realms, saying, "... And my Divine helpers, in the forms of the intelligences that come through my crystal skulls, have bonded with me in a way I could not have allowed before. I explicitly trust them."

In addition, Kathleen commented:

"So now I have a skull who says he/she was not carved on the earth, full of stories of our stellar heritage. Kalif, a contemporary carved skull with

Lemurian wisdom, and Jade an ancient skull, who, I believe, has been used in many different cultures, and has vast powers of transformation. She has definitely been a shamanic, alchemical and spiritual tool. My job as guardian is to take these skulls out for people to experience their beauty and wisdom. I love it!"

Her final statement is one that I would second because it supports my own beliefs about these wonderful mineral carvings:

"Lastly I would say that I am a crystal skull guardian because I know the Divine beings that work through my skulls, and I am here to take my skulls out to share with people. They are sacred, they are here to teach us that we are sacred, too."

Chapter Seven

HOW CRYSTAL SKULLS COMMUNICATE WITH US

My research into crystal skulls has clearly shown that they do, indeed, communicate with us. Some custodians of these carvings gain impressions from them. Several have said they suddenly acquire thoughts and feelings or as Ravenia Todd says, "I occasionally receive spontaneous inspirations . . . ," while in the presence of crystal skulls. Other people, including myself, channel their words through automatic writing. There are some who say they can definitely hear a crystal skull speaking to them. For Mark Loman it is a constant babble of skull voices. In addition, meditation and dreamwork are two further ways of being 'in touch' with these crystal friends. In my opinion, all of these forms of communication are viable. A crystal skull will 'speak' to each one of us in whatever way is best for our individual needs.

However, the question of whether it is the skull itself communicating or only other entities speaking through it remains unanswered. I believe that both scenarios are possible. Mark's labradorite skull, Morgan, definitely gives the impression of having a personality, as do my skull companions, Molmec, Lopa and Cheiron. Equally, Kathleen Murray's experience with Mahasamatman and the Galactic Masters, together with my findings about the Voladi through Rupel, would suggest that other beings utilize these carvings for making contact with us. Apparently, a crystal skull is a tool that creates a link between the physical plane and other dimensions, and this connection then enables conversation between them. My contact with the Voladi through Rupel was explained in the following manner two days after I received the information on the DNA realignment/attunement procedure:

> "I wish to tell you about ourselves and who we are. I am not the skull itself speaking to you, it is merely the device through which communication takes place. Think of it as a telephone receiver, yet it is much more. We can and do communicate with humans through the mineral quartz that is either remaining in its natural state or has been shaped in some manner by humans. But the skull shape is the most desirable, it accesses and transmits our words more readily, and it is within the human nature to accept a crystal skull speaking rather than a rock.
>
> We are the Voladi and we do not fully exist in the same dimension as that of humans. We are one of many collectives, which are observing and sometimes influencing your planet's existence. These other collectives also communicate with humans through crystal skulls and other mineral objects. The frequency of quartz is most conducive to our vibration, therefore, we confine ourselves to communicating with you only through that mineral. And, as you know, quartz is very

prolific within your planet, therefore, it follows that we have communicated with humans long and often, since their earliest times to your present days. Sometimes this has been through crystal skulls and at other times through anything that contains the mineral quartz within it. We prefer the object to be pure quartz, but the existence of other minerals or substances does not prevent our words from being received. These objects may be as small as a tiny pebble, or as large as a building, or even a mountain. Now, you begin to understand that we are everywhere, gently whispering to humans." 1

In Chapter Eight there is yet another example of crystal skulls being used by other dimensional entities in order to help us.

Meditation is often a very good way to make contact with a crystal skull. It is certainly the manner in which I began to learn about these amazing mineral friends. By sitting quietly with Suyan and later with Tol-Remy-Ran, I was given many insights into what is possible for anyone who becomes a crystal skull custodian. Today, it is a practice that I follow with each new skull that comes into my home. Some crystal skulls give visual images during meditation, as a way of sharing information. Others put actual words into the mind and field of perception. And yet other skulls communicate using both methods to convey what they want us to know. There are meditation exercises in Chapter Thirteen that can be followed, if you would like to 'talk' with your crystal skull.

Two of Mark Loman's skulls gave him some interesting information through this form of communication. While meditating with a newly acquired 4 lb. amethyst skull, named Samson, he heard the words, "We come from the Sacred Seven." Mark waited for more information, but none was given.

Almost a week later, he decided to ask his clear quartz skull, Denuvian, about the Sacred Seven. He sat quietly in meditation and was soon flying very high up over a black sea. Then he saw seven islands beneath him and on each island there was a huge pyramid. When relating the experience to me, he said the pyramids were "at least twenty times larger than anything existing today." Three sides of each pyramid were smooth, but the fourth side had a very large image of a head incorporated into it about two-thirds of the way down. Mark told me these seven heads and their faces were fashioned similarly to the stone carvings on Easter Island. He added that each one was wearing a box-type head-dress. There were steps leading from the ground up to the open mouth of each face, and white-robed people were climbing up the steps and entering the pyramids through these openings.

The next image that was given to him was inside one of the pyramids. It was a huge chamber with a massive hole in the center of its floor. Protruding up from this hole were three gigantic crystals that slanted inwards to form a tent-like appearance. Surrounding the crystals and in the space between them was what Mark described as "a blue light, energy vortex." The robed figures were lining up and taking turns to enter this blue light and bathe in it. They entered it from one side as people, but exited from the other side as "light beings." Then they quickly vanished "into thin air."

The scene in front of Mark changed and he was, once more, high above the islands. The next thing he saw was all seven pyramids exploding, and soon nothing was left other than "a blackened rubble." There was a great sense of a cataclysmic event having taken place. This ended his meditation with Denuvian.

From what he had been shown, Mark concluded that the Sacred Seven were the pyramids. Naturally, he was curious about where they had been located and what had happened to them. Therefore, two days later, he asked Denuvian about this. During this meditation, he was told rather than shown the answer to his question. Polaris was the name given to him. It was set up as a colony by "a civilization of nomadic, interdimensional gypsies," who visited Earth when she was young. This colony existed "on the pole, which was not frozen at that time." These beings used Earth's magnetic poles to generate the blue light energy, and this helped maintain their life force. It also facilitated their interdimensional travel by converting them into pure energy light beings. When the earth's polarity began to shift, it unstablized the seven vortices and they broke down. This then caused the destruction of the pyramid structures that Mark had been shown. There was a knock-on effect from this cataclysm. Land masses shifted, new continents were formed and the earth was plunged into an ice age. Denuvian ended this message about Polaris by informing Mark that evidence of the colony remains deeply buried in the ice and snow. This skull also intimated that, if global warming continues, this evidence will surface as the ice melts. Mark concluded the session with Denuvian by asking where these interdimensional beings came from, where they belonged. He was given this incongruous response: "Everywhere and nowhere." When Mark told me about his meditation with Denuvian, I asked whether he had been told that Polaris was at the North or South Pole, but he said only the words "the pole" were given to him.

In Chapter Eight there is much more information about the Sacred Seven, and it would appear that this was not the name for the seven pyramids that were shown to Mark within meditation.

When we meditate, our brains are functioning in what is known as "the alpha brain wave pattern." We also enter this state just before going to sleep, as we are waking up and when we day-dream. On two separate occasions, while in the alpha state, Mark has seen a crystal skull that he believes will be with him at some point in the future. He told me:

> "Another skull came to me last night, it was in that 'in between' state while I was still awake. She looked like nothing I'd seen before, very distinctive with deep eye sockets and very high nose holes. She seemed very old and was of some sort of quartz of an off-white, yellowish color. She had a perfect pyramid inside her forehead that was spinning slowly. She spoke very clearly and said she was on her way, and that her name was Isis. Also, that we had some serious work to do."

Several evenings later, Isis put in an appearance, again, and Mark was not the only one to see her this time:

> "This last vision was the strongest by far and came while I was sitting in bed and reading a book. Something distracted me from the page. Rhona, one of my kittens, was just staring straight at me and she was transfixed. Looking ahead, I saw Isis floating about two feet in front of me, approximately one foot above the bed. The image is so strong you feel that it would be possible to just reach out and pluck her straight from the air. Again, she says her name: "I am Isis. We have some serious work to do. Watch for me, I'm coming to you." Again, no information on where or how she is coming, but I will say I feel she is getting closer all the time. I am excited as she is the one who will cause profound changes in my life. She really is a strange looking skull, not like any I've seen before, so I will know her as soon as we meet."

Mark is convinced Isis will be with him one day and he is anxiously awaiting her arrival.

Crystal skulls also definitely communicate with us when we sleep. As previously mentioned, Lopa revealed its full name during a dream and it also urged me to work with all of my crystal skulls at this time. I was given the impression that some of the information held by each skull has an allotted time frame within which it can be shared. If I wait too long, I will miss this window of opportunity.

When Mark Loman took Morgan to bed with him, in a dream she showed him "an amazing cave full of skulls bathed in beautiful rainbow light." On another night she gave him some information about a friend's mother who was suffering from bone cancer. In the dream, Mark visited her in her home in Majorca. He explained:

> "She looked wonderful, if not a little strange, dressed in an iridescent frock with her long hair flowing. Her eyes and finger nails, which were very long, were made of the most vivid labradorite."

Mark felt the message of the dream was that this mineral would be helpful to her.

The next day he phoned his friend and told her to find a piece of labradorite and to have her mother wear or carry it. The friend bought her mother a necklace made of labradorite and she wore it until the time of her passing, several months later. Mark and I believe this mineral eased her suffering and gently guided her into the spirit realm.

Ravenia Todd also echoes my belief that crystal skulls communicate with us during sleep and impact upon our dreams:

> "One interesting 'ability' of many crystal skulls is that of affecting a person's dreams. I find that if I place a specific skull near to the head of the bed, it tends to affect my dreams. However, this seems to

depend on the skull, as some are more attuned to dreamwork than others. For example, I have one skull, Te-Ra, a near life-size citrine skull, that has great influence in the dream world. If I place Te-Ra near my pillow with the skull facing my direction, I am guaranteed wild, interesting, profound dreams. If the skull is not facing me, it doesn't impact on my dreaming. I have sporadically experimented with this over the years and it works every time! . . ."

Apparently, crystal skulls can communicate with us even when they are not in our presence. An example of this is a dream in which a skull is seen and then later appears in physical reality. As mentioned in the previous chapter, Ravenia dreamed of Belinda before she actually found her. She explained:

"Belinda is the first skull that came into my life. 'Out of the blue' one night I had a dream about a shiny, black skull that spoke to me. I wish my conscious mind could recall what was said. Whatever it was, the dream made an impact. I could not get the image of the black skull out of my mind for weeks afterwards. The features were very lifelike, not scary or grotesque. I had no interest in the human skull shape/symbol before the dream occurred. Some weeks afterwards I 'coincidentally' discovered a large and exquisite snowflake obsidian skull that was for sale. The features were very similar to the one in my dream, and although it was a lot of money to spend on a rock, I felt compelled to purchase the obsidian skull . . ."

In Chapter Four I said I dreamed about Cheiron the night before I purchased this skull. As the dream began, we had arrived at the warehouse, which looked like a very large shed with long trestle tables that held many different mineral specimens. In reality the next day, the warehouse proved to be completely different from my dream. As we approached the shed, a teenage girl came towards us. She was carrying a clear quartz skull that was extremely cloudy. The girl came up to me and made a point of showing me a number of tiny nicks all over the top of the cranium. In the dream, this apparent damage did not concern me. She offered the skull to me and the moment it touched my hands I knew that I wanted it. I stroked the top of the skull and, as I did so, I could feel the small indentations across it. I asked the girl for the skull's name and she spelled out the word "C-h-e-i-r-o-n." I looked closely at Cheiron and saw that all around the base of the lower jaw there was a garland of leaves carved into the quartz. I remember that I was impressed by the detail and artistry of this work. It seemed out-of-place on a crystal carving that had little clarity and was apparently damaged. I told the girl I would like to buy the skull, but she said it was her own and was not for sale. She quickly took Cheiron back from me and was gone. We entered the shed, but there were only a couple of small crystal skulls on the first table and they did not appeal to me. I felt extremely disappointed that I could not buy Cheiron, and at that point I woke up.

I have previously explained exactly what the tiny indentations were on the skull's cranium. They and much of the cloudiness have gone and I see this as a healing for Cheiron. I have speculated on the significance of the exquisitely carved leaves that, of course, are not physically present on this skull. Perhaps their message to me was a reminder that what may appear to be an ugly duckling can blossom into a beautiful swan? Also, Cheiron brings the ultimate healing—passage into the spirit plane. On the surface death may seem unattractive and unpleasant, yet it leads us to our true and radiant selves.

Sam Elliott has had three dreams in which crystal skulls appeared and with each there was a connection to Mark Loman. In one dream she actually heard his name spoken:

> "I am in a dark cavern. In front of me is a six foot tall skull made of clear quartz, it is not of or on this planet. It has lots of lightening coming out of it, none of which is dangerous to me. A loud voice says, "Mark!""

In a second dream she was shown a crystal skull that apparently will come to Mark one day, but as yet this has not happened. Sam explained:

> "I'm in a shop and I see a grapefruit-size, clear quartz skull on a counter top. It is dusty and only £40, a bargain. I look over the counter and am drawn to a tea chest, which has lots of old cloth in it. I go round and rummage through, and at the bottom is a human-size, amethyst skull priced at £225. I think the owners obviously don't know what they've got. I am then told clairaudiently that Mark will find this shop and the skulls, but he must only buy the large one and not haggle over the price."

During a third dream, Sam was working with an apophyllite pyramid:

> "This happened last night. I went inside the pyramid and saw a grapefruit-size, clear quartz skull called Starburst. It had a star of light coming out of its right eye and one tooth on the right side. It said it was coming to Mark, that someone would give it to Mark. It spoke very quietly and insistently and went, after I promised to tell Mark about it."

Mark found Starburst soon after Sam's dream. He went to a trade fair and, as he explained, the skull was obviously waiting there for him:

> "Starburst was the first thing I saw as I walked into the fair on Sunday. I spotted her before I'd even registered. She was about 50 feet away from the door and almost jumping up and down, winking away like a mad thing. I could see the starburst behind her eye even from that distance."

Another method of communication that a crystal skull will employ, when it is not physically with us, is through a photograph of itself. When these carvings are purchased from an outlet in another country, photographs of them are usually the only means by which the prospective buyer can browse and choose. People have reported experiencing a crystal skull 'speaking' to them when they observed its photographic image. There are even incidents of scenes being seen within the skull's still likeness.

I, myself, have encountered a crystal skull communicating with me through its photograph. This was the British Skull that is housed at the British Museum in London. It is a life-size, clear quartz skull that is similar in appearance to the Mitchell-Hedges Skull. In earlier years, this artifact was always on display, but more recently it has been stored away and is rarely exhibited. There were rumors that it scared people so much that it needed to be removed. Another theory is that there are doubts about its ancient authenticity, therefore, it is not on permanent display. Testing done on the skull a few years ago revealed jeweler's wheel markings on it, and these dated it as being carved post 1492 A.D. This would put it into the category of "old" not "ancient."

Between December 7, 2000 and February 11, 2001, the

skull was brought out of storage and displayed as part of the 'Human Image Exhibition.' My husband and I did not want to miss the opportunity of seeing this artifact, so in late January 2001 we visited the museum. The skull was positioned in a glass case, but this did not prevent me from receiving some impressions from it. I was told that it was extremely lonely and wanted to be out and about, doing esoteric work. It indicated that I could work with it from a distance, if I could find a picture of it somewhere. I also felt quite strongly that it was carved in recent times.

I did not tell my husband what I had been given. However, when we had looked at everything in the Exhibition, I asked him to go back to the skull and to stay in front of it for a short time in order to communicate with it. While he did this, I sat down on a bench and watched him stand by the glass case, staring at the skull. After a few minutes, he came over to me and reported that he felt this crystal skull was very sad and lonely. He added, "It really wants to be taken out of that case." I told him I had received exactly the same impressions. Before leaving the museum, we visited the gift shop and there I bought a post card with a photograph of the skull on one side.

A few days after our museum visit, I sat quietly with this photograph and 'tuned into' the skull. I was given the word Shala as being the name by which I can know it. Also, that its energy signature is androgynous. I then saw a man with dark, curly hair, who was wearing wire framed glasses. He looked to be about 35 and had a mustache and a short beard, both of which were sprinkled with odd, ginger hairs. The man's name was Frederick and he was the person who had carved this crystal skull. The date 1892 came into my mind.

I did no further work with Shala's photograph until about a month after our visit to the museum. On that day I was told I can send Shala etherically to anyone, anywhere, who needs healing, comfort and help. I sensed that this skull misses Frederick and this is a part of the sadness that surrounds it. Apparently, this is not unusual because bonding takes place between a crystal skull and its creator. However, when it gains a new custodian, this eases the unhappiness, providing the skull is shown love and respect and worked with in a positive manner. It bonds with its custodian.

Shala has never been able to bond with anyone beyond Frederick because it has always been regarded as a piece of property rather than a well-loved companion and helper. This crystal skull has been viewed with curiosity, fear, dislike and even disinterest. It has been highly valued for its possible historical and cultural worth, but never treasured for its spiritual gifts. When I have completed this book, I hope to do more in-depth work with Shala by means of its photograph.

Soon after our visit to the museum, Mark Loman and Sam Elliott attended the Exhibition, as did Joshua Shapiro, who was in the UK at that time. Each of these people felt the skull was sad and wanted to be doing work rather than being stored away. Both Sam and Mark also believe the skull is not ancient.

It is possible there are many other ways that crystal skulls can speak to us. Perhaps one of these is through the Tarot cards. Sam Elliott has two small crystal skulls, but her passion is working with crystal spheres. However, she has discovered that she can link with, and gain information about, a skull by consulting the Tarot cards while 'tuning into' it. As mentioned before, it was Sam who told me that Cheiron would help the terminally ill pass into spirit. She gained this information while doing a Tarot card reading for this skull.

Sam also conducted similar card readings for some of my other crystal skulls. I gave her their names and she sent me her impressions in an email. Prior to the readings, she knew nothing about these skulls. The first one she linked with was

Molmec, and she told me, "He is chatty and assists with public speaking, likes to travel and can assist people change their emotional and mental outlook, promotes a sense of peaceful confidence." As previously explained, Molmec has frequently been with me when I have spoken to, and taught, members of the general public. He definitely likes to be taken out and about, and I am sure his gift of healing brings both a positive emotional and mental outlook.

The second skull Sam gave a reading for was Rupel. She saw this one as being:

> "A spiritual teacher/advisor, deals with life as a whole and has a strong moon aspect. Fosters true love and wants to bring people together in a world peace kind of way. Can have a changeable personality and be forceful, if needed. Will change the way you work."

I can certainly agree that Rupel is a "spiritual teacher/adviser" whose realignment/attunement procedure helps people progress and, therefore, be more inclined to want a peace-filled world. This skull can be changeable. Sometimes it is silent, yet at other times I can easily channel its words through automatic writing. However, a "changeable personality" could also explain Rupel's androgynous energy signature

Another crystal skull Sam read the cards for was Tol-Remy-Ran. About him she wrote:

> "A communicator and star child, personally happy but has a seed of pain. Has traveled a very long way and was quite unwell in a very dark place. This has given courage, frankness and risk taking, very creative."

Tol-Remy-Ran has often communicated with me, both when I am awake and sleeping. In addition, there is something off-world about him. The very first time I held him, he showed me what appeared to be an alien landscape. He can also be seen as "very creative" because he is the initiator of the exercises that are given later in this book. I have not, however, been aware of his "seed of pain." Perhaps he keeps it well hidden or, maybe, he has absorbed this vibration from Lopa. From the very first day of Lopa's arrival, I have always placed him next to Tol-Remy-Ran. They seemed to be comfortable together. Being "unwell in a very dark place" would explain why Lopa felt and appeared so negative when I first saw him. I can believe that Tol-Remy-Ran has chosen to shoulder some of Lopa's pain.

Yet another means of crystal skull communication may have been experienced by Ravenia Todd. While working in close proximity to such a large number of crystal skulls, she has become aware of a sound they are making. Her following observation is thought provoking:

> "... Another interesting phenomenon that I cannot explain, but I do associate with the skulls, is a high pitched, monotone whistling. I personally believe it is brought about by having a large number of skulls in a small area. In our Skull Room we have several hundreds of skulls. The Skull Room is where the whistling tends to happen, though I have also heard it in a Denver hotel room, while doing a gemstone show with several hundreds of skulls with us in the room.
>
> The whistling imparts an eerie, primal appeal. It sounds like a high pitched monotone. When it starts up, it fades in, and when it ends, it fades out. It never seems to start or end abruptly. I cannot explain what happens to cause the whistling, however, I feel that the many crystalline energies that exist around these skulls are responsible."

Apart from their communication with us, there is also the possibility of crystal skulls talking to one another. Maybe this whistling sound is the means by which they do this.

1. Marion Webb-De Sisto, *Soul Wisdom, Volume One*, p. 209-210.

Chapter Eight

THE SACRED SEVEN

Several months after being shown the seven pyramids by Denuvian, Mark Loman began a study course on channeling and automatic writing. This training encouraged him to attempt the latter while meditating with a crystal skull. On this occasion, the one he chose was Kujo. Carved at 'Raven's Roost' from a high grade, Brazilian clear quartz and weighing 4.50 lbs., this skull presents a projective energy signature. Kujo is a beautifully carved specimen with drilled nostrils and hollowed-out cheek and jaw bones. There is plenty of rainbow irising and many wonderful veils within him. The following is the message Mark received from Kujo through automatic writing:

> "We are connected, again. I have traveled through time to be with you, again. The work we can do is infinite. The wisdom of the old ones is in us. The skulls are your allies and friends, not just tools.

> They represent the combined wisdom of all dimensions of existence. They show you portals to these so you can gain knowledge and understanding of what is, what can be and what is gone. They will teach you well, if you are willing to learn. Use seven skulls in a pattern to make the Sacred Seven configuration. Sit within and feel the power and energies flow through you."

Mark was then shown the layout/mandala below with the skulls facing inwards:

$$O\ 1$$

$$4\ O \qquad O\ 5$$

$$2\ O \qquad O\ 3$$

$$6\ O \qquad O\ 7$$

Several days later, Mark decided to set up this pattern on the floor of his living room with seven of his crystal skulls. Once they were in place, he then sat down in the center of the configuration. He had a notepad and pen with him and quickly channeled this message:

> "We are the Sacred Seven ascended masters and teachers, here to expand your consciousness. Feel the vortex power we create. Seven masters, seven star systems, seven wonders. Workers of light and energy. You feel dizzy and sick. We are clearing blocks and any old karmic attachments to make you ready for the new work we have in mind for you. Marion needs to do the same meditation with seven of her skulls. We will work through them as we work through these.

"My name is Megazor, chief spokesman for the Sacred Seven and also the oldest of our kind. Laylamar, Razimar, Yozell, Matrelli, Ozkoth and Odesseas. We travel far, but fast, we give help to those who wish it. Each master teaches a different talent or subject.

That is enough for now, we can tell the energy is making you feel odd. Do this, again, soon. The changes we have made to your etheric body are subtle, yet are necessary to help you receive us more clearly. Rest now, be at peace."

Now, it was obvious to Mark that the Sacred Seven were beings who were making contact with him through his crystal skulls, and not the seven pyramids that he had been previously shown. He thanked them for their words and quickly telephoned me to tell me what had happened. Mark said he experienced the sensation of sitting in the middle of a strong vortex of energy and that it made him feel quite dizzy. He suggested that I try this same layout, just as the Sacred Seven had recommended.

I did this the next day, using seven of my own crystal skulls. From what Mark had told me, I concluded that the energy within the pattern of skulls would be very ungrounding. Therefore, I decided to hold what I consider to be a very grounding skull while sitting in the center of the other seven. I chose Nedril to be with me. This is a 4 lb. red jasper skull with an androgynous energy vibration. It was carved at 'Raven's Roost' and, like Kujo, has drilled nostrils and hollowed-out jaw and cheek bones. I believe Nedril did help me to remain grounded because at no time did I feel dizzy or light-headed. However, there was a sensation of gentle rocking, at first, and this then became an equally gentle bouncing up and down and from side to side.

I was shown a scene of huge ice mountains cascading

down into a jet black sea. There was a strong impression that this was not a place on Earth. Then I saw a Native American man whom I recognized as being the same individual I had seen several years ago within a meditation. During that earlier session, I was told this was an image of myself in another lifetime, a very long time ago. In this present meditation, the man had a large, beautiful, white feather attached to the front of his raven-colored hair. The quill point was somehow secured just above the left temple and the rest of the feather diagonally followed the contour of his hair towards the back of his head. I heard the name "White Feather" and felt sure that is the English translation of my name in that other lifetime.

No other scenes came to me so I decided to ask for a message from the Sacred Seven. I had taken paper and pen into the layout, therefore, I was ready to channel their words. This is what I was given through automatic writing:

> "We take you to other times and other places. Journey with us, we are one. This is a place of solitude, yet many are with us. We are a portal to what may have been, what could have been and what was. We are a portal to what may be, what could be and what will be. Little one, we are the portal to ALL THAT IS, the absolute NOW, the Alpha and the Omega.
>
> Just as Rupel adjusts and aligns your vibrational flow so that you can more easily progress with your planet, we are the vessel that transports you along your path. For those who are not acquainted with Rupel's gifts or the level of his vibrations, we will adjust and align their subtle energy to an appropriate level for our work. Those who have received blessings from Rupel and the higher realms are more ready to journey with us to their soul agreements and dimensional progression.

Help all to journey with us so that we can align, teach, comfort and nurture them through their days of physical existence. Little one, return to us when you are able. We are the Sacred Seven."

When I ended the session, I thought it had lasted about twenty minutes. However, on checking the clock, I realized that almost an hour had passed. It would appear that time is distorted within the Sacred Seven layout.

A few days later, I encouraged my husband to sit inside this pattern of crystal skulls. He chose different ones from those that formed my layout and he did not take an extra skull into the center with him. I stayed close by and, occasionally, asked him to tell me what he could see. My husband's inner vision is always very strong when he closes his eyes. He did not know what I had seen, yet, in the beginning, there appeared to be a Native American connection. The first scene he described was of many, many buffalo that were stampeding. He could hear the thunder of their hooves and felt pulled by their swift motion. There was also dust rising and swirling around. The buffalo were being hunted, but he could not tell me whether the hunters were White or Native Americans.

Then he was quiet for a while except to tell me that his legs felt cold. Later, he described a life-size, smoky quartz skull that he could see in a room in a building. It was on a pedestal and he believed the building was an auction place in Louisiana. There were other crystal skulls on a table, but none were as large as the smoky quartz. Then he was outside of the building and there were two men, discussing what they would bid on the skull. He said this was not the present time because the men were dressed in the fashion of the mid 1800s. He repeated several times, "This is so real," and added that he had a sharp pain in his temples.

Once again, he was silent and this lasted for about fifteen

minutes. Towards the end of this time, I saw that he began to look extremely upset. I suggested that he end the session and this he did. After the skulls were cleared away, I told him I had noticed he was becoming distressed. I asked if this was because of the pain he felt in his head. He assured me it was not, but said he had seen bombs exploding everywhere and this was very upsetting. Finally, I questioned my husband about how long he thought he had sat in the middle of the skulls. His answer only stated a third of the actual time he was there.

Another person who has tried the Sacred Seven layout is Sue Bouvier. As she only had two skulls at the time, the other five points of the pattern were marked with crystals. Mark Loman had told her he was given the impression that crystals could be substituted for skulls. Knowing I was writing about the Sacred Seven, Sue forwarded to me the following account of her experience:

> "I laid down inside the skull formation and very quickly found myself flying up into the universe. I could actually feel myself flying. The sky all around me was deep blue with thousands and thousands of sparkling stars.
> Then I saw a pyramid and saw myself enter the pyramid. It was not an Egyptian pyramid. I felt it was earlier than an Egyptian pyramid. I was standing in front of a crystal ball, which was on a beige, stone stand. There were two men standing slightly behind me, either side of me.
> I looked into the crystal ball and saw myself inside another pyramid. This pyramid was Egyptian. I had long black hair to my waist and was dressed in a long dress of, I think, turquoise. I seemed to be about to do some kind of ritual. I asked what was I seeing and was told that this was part of another dimension of my life, but it was not the dimension I am in now.

This vision faded quickly and I saw myself inside a teepee. There was an Indian chief in front of me. I am sure he was White Eagle, my Indian guide, although he had on the most magnificent white feather head dress. He was talking to me, but I did not know what he was saying. I asked what was the reason for this vision and, again, they told me I was being shown another dimension of myself, but not the dimension I am in now.

I then moved from this scene and found myself standing inside a stone circle in a field. I feel sure it was the Roll Right Stones in Oxfordshire, although I haven't been to them for over thirty years, so I cannot be sure. I just feel it was the Roll Rights. I seemed to be giving a talk of some kind. I could not see the people I was talking to, but I could sense there were many sitting, listening. I did not understand this vision, either, and asked what it represented. I was told this is a future dimension of myself, but not the one I am in now. Then everything went black and I felt myself lying on the floor of my lounge. I knew that I would see nothing else.

During this experience I had no concept of time. The only sensation I felt was heat traveling throughout my body. I felt very hot. As I got up from the layout, I said I did not really understand the reason why I was shown what I had seen. And certainly didn't understand the reference to the Roll Right Stones, other than, once again, the vision of teaching others about, in particular, Druidry and, to a lesser extent, Paganism..."

Again, there is a Native American overtone to a part of this Sacred Seven session, and Sue also lost a sense of time while lying in the layout.

About two weeks after sitting inside the seven skull layout, Mark Loman decided to try a second session. During this time, he saw "a spinning vortex with the symbol of a triangle inside it." The three lines of this geometric figure were spiraling outwards. Like my husband, he also experienced coldness in his legs. He received three lines of automatic writing and then felt a strong desire to drum. Mark owns a beautiful Native American drum, which he often plays. He thought his drumming lasted around ten minutes, but later realized he had played the drum for about an hour and a half. After putting aside this instrument, the automatic writing continued. The following is the complete message that he received:

> "We are the font of all knowledge. We will share with you so you may share with others. You will make an excellent voice channel, when fully adjusted. (At this point Mark played his drum) We are the Cherokee spirit fathers. We taught the ancestors much. They are not only the crystal keepers, but are the true earth keepers and healers.
>
> At this time, we need more keepers of secrets as the old customs and bloodlines are running thin. We will choose people of all nationalities and backgrounds who are suitable for receiving the message of healing and hope. We strive to heal the earth and her many families. A new season in Earth's future is drawing ever closer and we all need to be ready for the dawn of a new epoch, a new era. Much adjustment is needed.
>
> With purity of thought and no malice, go forth and speak our message. Help others see the importance. Be ready."

Mark asked if there was anything he should do for his adjustment, and was told:

"No, we do all the necessary adjustments for you. Sit quietly and let it happen. You may feel nothing at all. Every time you enter the mandala, you will be adjusted and fine tuned."

He then questioned whether there was any further information to be given within the automatic writing. "No, not now." was the reply.

At the time of writing this chapter, I have not sat inside a Sacred Seven pattern of crystal skulls, again. I do, however, intend to pursue and research this fascinating exercise for both myself and other people. Mark and I have agreed to give a Sacred Seven workshop at the 2002 May Festival of Holistic Living. During a part of this event, we will place the workshop participants inside a layout of seven, life-size crystals skulls and allow them to enjoy the experience. I anticipate some interesting feedback.

I am not yet certain of the full significance of this crystal skull layout, but it appears to have a strong Native American connection. The pattern also seems to create a field of energy in which people can observe different time frames and other places. These could possibly be past or future lives for the observer, but I do not think they will always be such. According to what has been channeled during a Sacred Seven session, some adjustments to a participant's energy vibration may take place, as well. I would see this as a form of healing. In addition, there is the loss of time that we have all experienced while sitting within the mandala of seven crystal skulls. Time is an illusion of the physical plane and, when we enter an energy vortex such as this, we are no longer fully established in a three-dimensional existence. We are accelerated and exist somewhere between the physical and the spiritual. When we leave the layout and re-enter the tangible world, there is a stepping-down of our energy vibration. We also realize that illusionary time has continued its passage while we were gone.

As to the identity of the Sacred Seven, more research is needed to understand who they are and why they are making themselves known to us. Rupel has indicated that a number of collective consciousnesses have watched over and guided the human race. It would appear that Mark Loman and his crystal skull, named Kujo, have introduced us to yet another of these composites of other worldly, powerful benefactors.

Chapter Nine

CRYSTAL SKULLS & THE UNIVERSAL LIGHT GRIDWORK

In Chapter Four, I referred to the Earth Changes for which there have been a number of predictions. These changes are also indicative of the progression that our planet is currently experiencing, and this transformation has everything to do with something known as the Universal Light Gridwork. The information regarding this network of light was given to me by my angelic guides back in 1992, and in *Soul Wisdom, Volume One* I explained about it. The following extract from that book highlights the functioning and necessity of the Gridwork:

> "Our planet is an important energy point or vortex on the energy network of the universe, which is known as the Universal Light Gridwork. It may help the reader to think of this gridwork as the glue that holds the physical universe together, although it, itself, does

not exist on the physical level. All 'heavenly bodies,' suns, planets and moons possess their own individual gridworks, but only certain planets are also key points on the Universal Light Gridwork. They are the ones that contain within their physical makeup a very high percentage of the mineral quartz. Every few million years, Earth and the other focal planets upgrade their energy frequencies in order to maintain the increasingly higher energy level of the network. This is a slow process, it does not happen in a short space of physical time. However, it seems to be debatable as to whether the upgrading planets create a higher frequency within the gridwork or if the increase in gridwork energy, forces the planets to upgrade. The reader can look upon this as akin to the age-old question—which came first, the chicken or the egg?

At times, when an upgrading is due, there has either been a delay or an actual downgrading of one or more of the planets' energy fields. This has been brought about partly by the adverse actions of the planet's inhabitants, but mostly by the negativity of the group thinking. Earth has had this happen more than once, and during a downgrading, her own personal gridwork has slowly dimmed to the point of being switched off. Any time this happens, it places our planet in grave jeopardy of literally breaking apart. This does not happen overnight, it takes many millennia, but as the expanse of time slowly passes, Earth's internal structure, her true self, begins to disintegrate. Ultimately, this would then be followed by the ending of her structural self. This, in turn, would gravely affect the Universal Light Gridwork. Therefore, it becomes imperative both for Earth and the Gridwork to rapidly upgrade before it is too late.

Earth had been in a downgrade mode for several

thousand years, and it was only about halfway through the twentieth century that her own gridwork was switched back on. Her required upgrading was well overdue by a number of millennia, and so, she has been undergoing a greatly accelerated upgrade, which has been taking place since the late 1960's. Armed with this knowledge, it is easier to understand why there has been such a rapid swing towards esoteric matters for many people across the planet within the past twenty-five to thirty years.

Whenever Earth is getting ready for an upgrading, many facet souls are attracted to incarnate on her in order to help or hinder her progression . . ."1

One of the guides I channel is the planet on which we live, the Earth Mother, and in several of her messages she has identified certain people as being those who are here to help with her upgrading. This information has usually been given within a channeled reading for the individual. Following this identification, the Earth Mother, also known as Orabal, explains how the individual can aid her progression. Sometimes, this is merely to continue actions that the person is already doing. At other times, instructions are given for new projects. These can be as simple as making closer contact with nature, as in meditating in the countryside or at the beach, or becoming involved in growing plants and working the soil. For other people, Orabal's requests are more unusual. Some are asked to walk what she calls her "energy pathways" and which I believe are ley lines. Others are instructed to work with her divas and nature sprites. I, myself, have carried out several actions that Orabal has asked me to perform. These include burying crystals in certain locations and along her energy pathways, as well as taking specific crystals into the center of standing stones. I have been told by Orabal that these huge stone structures are her "energy centers" or chakras. The crystals strengthen and balance the energy vibration of these powerful circles. To most people these may seem to be unusual practices, but they have brought me a sense of peace and the hope that I am making a positive difference. In today's fast-paced, technologically-inspired world it is also very refreshing to be able to do something that does not require a computer, a mobile phone, or a fax machine. It is amazing how powerful these actions feel, the energy that surrounds them is almost tangible.

Perhaps some of the above practices are already being carried out by you. If this is so, be aware that you are doing these things on the guidance of the Earth Mother. You may not know that she is prompting you, you may not have even considered the possibility that our planet is a sentient being. However, I and an increasing number of people believe this to be true. We also recognize the close link that exists between humans and their home planet. She is our Earth Mother who needs our love and support, and who continually gives these blessings back to us.

Within the past thirty years there has been a growing awareness of the need to use environmental-friendly products, to recycle trash and to replenish the forests, but we have a long way to go in order to reclaim an ecological balance in the twenty-first century. By striving to re-establish this balance, we not only demonstrate our desire to survive, but also our love for the beautiful planet that is our home. If you are already taking part in this resurgence of being environmentally responsible, I applaud you and, perhaps, you may decide to add some of the above mentioned actions to your existing ones. And, if by reading this book, you feel guided to purchase a large, clear quartz skull, you will become the custodian of a tool that is already helping to ensure our planet's progression.

The majority of the crystal skulls that have chosen to live in my home were carved from the Quartz Family and eleven of these are clear quartz. However, only one is life-size, weighing 10 lbs. and presenting an androgynous energy signature. This is Py-Ratti, a beautiful and powerful skull that was carved from Brazilian quartz at 'Raven's Roost.' It has the classic Raven, hollowed-out cheek and jaw bones and displays many rainbows and faceted structures inside itself. Upon seeing a photograph of this skull, I recognized its potential to be a unique and special companion for me within my esoteric work. The first time I touched Py-Ratti, the Reiki energy in my hands was stimulated and began to flow, and this has continued to happen each time I hold this skull. This indicates to me that Py-Ratti is a healing tool that will enhance any Reiki sessions that I give to others. I also believe this skull will be helpful within the passing of Reiki attunements. During one of my early meditations with Py-Ratti, it told me that it wanted to be one of the crystal skulls for the Sacred Seven workshop in the upcoming 2002 May Festival of Holistic Living.

However, I am not writing about Py-Ratti because of these attributes. It appears in this chapter because of the information it has given to me about the Universal Light Gridwork. Before purchasing this life-size crystal skull, I had become aware that there was a link between these mineral carvings and the Gridwork. This was shared with me by Tol-Remy-Ran during one of my numerous meditations with him. Following this disclosure, I was very curious to learn more, but neither Tol-Remy-Ran nor any other crystal skull would elaborate on this piece of information, no matter how many times I asked for it within later meditations. Then Py-Ratti arrived and I quickly gained a sense of it holding a wealth of wisdom that it wanted to teach. Therefore, I asked it to tell me how crystal skulls are connected to the Universal Light Gridwork.

I was shown the most gigantic clear quartz crystal that is embedded deeply in the heart of our planet. As I observed this huge, mineral specimen, it appeared to exist on the physical plane, yet I knew that much of itself and its properties are functioning at the etheric level. I cannot estimate the size of this amazing crystal, but I feel sure it is much greater than any that has ever been mined. Emanating from this crystal was a massive column of swirling, pulsating divine Light that pushed its way up through all the layers of the planet and stretched out into the vastness of space. Its movement continued on until it connected with other similar columns that together formed an intricate, radiant lattice-work across the universe. Although I could see the earthly column and the Light network, I knew they exist within the higher realms and not in the physical. They form the Universal Light Gridwork that is only revealed when it is necessary for us to believe in its existence.

Next, Py-Ratti made me aware that any large, clear quartz skulls that already exist on or in our planet are feeding energy to the earthly column of divine Light. Again, this is taking place at the etheric level and it is a never-ending action, no matter where the skulls are or whose keeping they are within. This means that any ancient clear quartz skulls, such as the Mitchell-Hedges one, as well as those just carved recently, are all contributing to this all important act. I was also told that smaller, clear quartz skulls, in turn, feed energy to their larger, fellow skulls, therefore, they, too, have their value in the Light network.

As mentioned in the beginning of this chapter, Earth is presently undergoing a rapid upgrading, and perhaps the information Py-Ratti gave to me explains why so many more crystal skulls are being fashioned and sort after. People, who collect these wonderful companions, are attracted to many that have been carved from various minerals, but most of these individuals have at least one that is a clear quartz skull. If you were to ask them about this particular one, they would tell you it is very special and does appear to be more finely tuned to esoteric matters. This may well be due to its place within the functioning of the Universal Light Gridwork.

So, if you are, or in the future you become, the custodian of a large, clear quartz skull, guard it well. Treat it with the love and respect that it deserves and do not allow it to come into the possession of those who would abuse its divinity. In later chapters, there are a number of suggestions of how you can ensure that it does not become damaged, lost, or misused.

1.   Marion Webb-De Sisto, *Soul Wisdom, Volume One*, p. 155-156.

PART TWO

Taking Care of Crystal Skulls

Chapter Ten

CHOOSING A CRYSTAL SKULL

After reading these stories about the various crystal skulls, perhaps you have decided that you would like to buy one. There are thousands of them in existence from which you can choose, and more are being carved every day. They are being fashioned from many different minerals and in a wide range of styles and sizes. I have an opal skull that only measures 1.5 cms. from front to back. In comparison, Goliath, a clear quartz skull presently in Raven Youngman's keeping, is believed to be the largest specimen, weighing in at 91.50 lbs. and measuring 15 ins. from front to back. However, the majority of these mineral carvings that you can purchase are much more moderately sized.

Choosing the right skull for you should not be a difficult task. Obviously, money will play a part in the decision making, and be prepared to pay a generous amount for your carved skull. Even a small one can be costly, and those that are life-size are usually very expensive. The high cost of crystal skulls is due to a number of factors. These include the skill and precision required in the carving process, also the grade and availability of the raw mineral specimen. In addition, the size of the mineral before carving takes place is about three times that of the final piece, and you are paying for the total specimen, including what is discarded.

If the price restricts your choice, do not think you are gaining less than what you need, if the skull you purchase is quite small. In my years of experience with the mineral kingdom, I have learned that we are given whichever crystal helpers are appropriate for our own development. There is also the belief that you do not pick a mineral specimen, but that it actually chooses you. A good rule to remember is that what appears to be less, is not, and sometimes may be more. A small tumble stone has within it the same divinity as that of a large crystal, therefore, it is equally as powerful. The same holds true for crystal skulls. In addition, many large mineral specimens, whether reshaped or left natural, are what I consider to be community rather than personal spiritual tools. They are here to help, to heal and to interact with many people instead of just one individual.

You can usually find crystal skulls for sale at metaphysical fairs and holistic festivals, on stands that are selling crystals and mineral specimens. Some crystal and New Age stores may also have a selection of them. It is a good idea to take some bubble wrap with you when you go to buy your crystal skull. Some retailers will package your purchase with plenty of paper, but many use a minimum of packing materials. You do not want your skull to become damaged before you have even begun to work with it. It is also possible to buy crystal skulls via the Internet, and this is how I have acquired the vast majority of my crystal skull collection. Keep in mind the fact that you will be making your choice from photographs and that these may not always give you a true impression of the skulls on offer. Also, only buy from reputable websites.

Further more, you should expect to pay for packaging, insurance and shipping, when making this type of purchase.

Before going to the festival, the store, or surfing the Net, take a few minutes to sit quietly and reflect on your reasons for wanting to buy a crystal skull. Are you planning to scry with it or is it to be of help with your own spiritual development? Perhaps you are a therapist who is looking for a crystal skull that will oversee and enhance your holistic practice. Maybe you have several mineral specimens that have been carved into spheres, obelisks, wands and animals, and you want to add a skull to your collection. Whatever the reason, during these minutes of silence send out a mental message of your specific requirement. Ask that the right crystal skull for your individual need will be available to you when you go to the festival, to the store, or when you go online. Make this request in a sincere and undemanding manner to the Divine, to the angels and to your spirit guides. If you do not have a specific reason for buying a crystal skull, but nevertheless feel drawn to these mineral carvings, then ask to be given the one that is appropriate for you.

Remember that outside of the physical plane there is no time, therefore, there is the possibility that your crystal skull will not be waiting for you on your first attempt to find it. However, do not become discouraged, you have made your request and it will be answered when the time is right. This may happen when you least expect it. Your crystal skull may arrive as an unexpected gift from a family member or friend. You may visit another town and, while wandering through a shopping mall, you discover a metaphysical store that sells crystal skulls. Knowing that you like crystals, a neighbor may pass on to you a mineral and gemstone catalogue that s/he received in the mail. On one of the pages is a display of mineral carvings, including a crystal skull. When we ask something of the Divine, it is invariably given to us, but not always in the way we expect or even want. So, be very careful what you ask of the higher realms because it will surely occur. Be very specific and have patience.

When you are in the crystal store, at the holistic festival, or browsing through the online retailer's stock, you may not be certain which is the right skull for you. Perhaps several crystal skulls are within the price range that you can afford or you feel equally attracted to two or three that are fashioned from different minerals. Is the rose quartz or the clear quartz the one you should be buying? Do you choose the larger or the smaller skull? You can afford to pay for either one. If you find yourself in this dilemma, take a moment to close your eyes and silently ask to be shown the one that is appropriate for your specific need. As you open your eyes, one of the skulls should catch your attention in some way. It may appear to smile at you or just seem to reflect the light in a more twinkling manner than the others. There should be something that now attracts you even more to this particular skull because you are being shown that it is the right one for you. This will also hold true when looking at photographs rather than the actual crystal skulls. Some retailers will allow you to hold mineral specimens before making a choice. Check with him or her whether this is something you can do. If given permission, hold whichever skulls you are trying to choose between, one at a time. By making physical contact with each skull, you should also get a sense of which one is the correct choice. You may experience a sense of peace, or warmth, or joy, when holding the right one.

For the few individuals who may remain uncertain which skull to choose after trying the methods I have suggested, I recommend that they rely on instinct, make a choice and just trust. As previously stated, I believe we are always provided with the appropriate mineral specimens to support our soul growth.

Once you have brought your crystal skull home or it has been delivered to you, there are a few things that you need to do before you can function together. As I said in Chapter Two, it is very important to cleanse all crystals and mineral specimens when they first come into our possession. Once that has been done, there are a couple of other procedures that I recommend for working safely and harmoniously with the mineral kingdom. These processes are discussed at length in the next chapter.

Chapter Eleven

CLEANSING, DEDICATING & TUNING

In my opinion the animal, plant and mineral kingdoms can all be influenced by both positive and negative energy that, in turn, will either benefit or damage them. Crystals enhance, magnify and focus the energy, which passes through them, and they also retain a residue of that energy within them. Therefore, it is of the utmost importance to ensure that any negative energy, which may be passing through or remaining in a crystal skull, is removed as quickly as possible. Before discussing some of the ways of removing this energy, it is helpful to understand how any type of mineral specimen can become 'dirty' or in need of cleansing. The following are some of the more common causes of negativity within crystals:

- mining, particularly by means of blasting—this is considered extremely traumatic for minerals.

- minerals having grown near or on a negative ley line—there has been some speculation on the effects of negative ley lines on humans, but not on minerals.
- negative events having happened on the surface above where the minerals grew—battles, massacres, etc. or any evil act played out within a location some distance above the 'home' of minerals. The negative energy from the event would not only cling to the ground surface, but would also seep far down into the planet, pass through the minerals located there and some of it would become trapped within them.
- bartering—whether between the mine owner and the wholesaler, the wholesaler and the retailer, or the retailer and the customer, this can create negative energy. The minerals in question would be close by or even in view of the individuals bartering and, where there is disagreement over money, there is negativity.
- intentional misuse—there are individuals who, understanding the power of the mineral kingdom, deliberately tap into that force by using a mineral specimen to enhance, magnify and focus their evil thoughts and actions.
- unintentional misuse—some people may not realize the potential that lies within minerals. If any are nearby when they are thinking or acting upon their negative intentions towards others, then those minerals will pick up some of that negativity.
- healing and therapeutic situations—clients release physical, emotional and mental pain when they receive healing, and this is a form of negativity. If any type of mineral, including a crystal skull, is being used as part of the healing or therapeutic modality, it will absorb some of that adverse energy.

In the following examples, if a crystal skull or any mineral specimen is in the same physical area as the occurrences given, the resulting effect on the specimen will be detrimental:

- long-term illness and death—when someone is long-term sick or dying, there is pain and unhappiness associated with this event and this can be seen as negativity.
- unhappy or negatively thinking/feeling people—a person who is sad, depressed, or of a pessimistic disposition, creates negative energy.
- unhappy, stressful, upsetting, frightening, arguing, and/or violent situations—any of these happenings will cause a negative atmosphere.
- unpleasant paranormal events—if a building, a room, or any area is subject to hauntings and spirit attachments that are not of a positive nature, then negativity is present.
- dirty surroundings—when a place is not physically clean, this generates negative energy.

Finally, it is known that the mineral amethyst, which is a member of the Quartz Family, has a natural tendency to attract and store negative energy within itself. Therefore, if you own a skull that has been carved from this mineral, it will need cleansing on a regular basis.

There are many ways to cleanse a crystal skull and if you try several of them, you will be able to decide which is the most practical and easy for you. A knowledge of the Mohs Scale of Hardness is also essential to ensure that the cleansing process being used does not damage the skull. Frederick Mohs (1773-1839) was a German mineralogist who defined the hardness of minerals by means of a scale from 1 (softest) to 10 (hardest). An example of his scale can be found at the back of this book. In general terms, methods that involve placing the skull in water, salt water, or sea salt are unsuitable for minerals that rank less than 7. Many skulls are carved from the Quartz Family, e.g. clear, smoky, snowy and rose quartz, amethyst, citrine, ametrine, jasper, aventurine and tigereye. This family of minerals is ranked 7, therefore, there will be no harm done from placing specimens of it in water and/or sea salt. However, other skulls have been fashioned from softer minerals, e.g. malachite (3.5-4), fluorite (4), lapis lazuli (5-5.5), hematite (5-6), labradorite (6) and obsidian (6-6.5) and they should not be cleansed in this manner. The best way to ensure that you do not damage your crystal skull, while cleansing it, is to invest in a small handbook on minerals that includes the hardness number for each one that is featured. This book can then become a reference guide as to which cleansing method is most appropriate for your skull.

As soon as a new crystal skull is in your possession, it is important to cleanse it, even if you are not aware of any negativity within it. If it is not necessary, you will do no harm to it, and it is very possible that the cleansing is needed. Before using any of the methods below, affirm that the negativity that you are removing from your crystal skull is transmuted to the Divine/Goddess/Great Spirit/God/etc. so that it may reach its highest, positive form.

Using Sound:

- Tibetan singing bowls, bells, cymbals, or tuning forks—hold a few inches above the skull and make sound by hitting, striking, etc. several times.
- chanting, singing, or reciting poems—hold the skull while doing these.
- place on a piano or an electric organ—be careful that the vibration, when the instrument is being played, does not dislodge the skull and cause it to fall.
- play tapes/CDs of classical music, New Age music, or

sounds of nature, e.g. birdsong, waterfalls, whale songs, etc.—place the skull in the proximity of the music or sounds.

*Using Other Crystals:**

- place on an amethyst bed—in order to avoid scratches and damage to the skull, place and remove it carefully and gently, especially if the skull is made from a softer mineral than quartz.
- place in a circle of cleansed crystals—use those that are of a similar size to the skull.
- place in a circle of cleansed skulls—position the surrounding skulls facing in towards the skull to be cleansed.

* not to be used if crystal skull is very 'dirty' or has been greatly misused because it may infect the other crystals or skulls.

Using Nature, The Earth Mother & The Plant Kingdom:

- place in a bed of dried flower petals—this works particularly well with rose petals.
- place in a bed of sage leaves, cedar chips, or sweetgrass—if none of these are readily available, but you have smudge sticks, break one apart and use its contents because these are usually made from sage and/ or sweetgrass.
- bury in the garden—place a marker in the event you forget where the skull is buried.
- bury in a pot of soil, peat, or sand—again, place a marker so that the pot is not used for a plant.
- place in full moonlight—even if the moon is hidden behind the clouds, the full moon energy will have a positive effect on the skull.

- place in bright sunlight **—a window-sill facing East will bring the healing rays of the morning sun, as well as heat that is less intense.
- hang in a net in a tree or bush, allowing the breeze to cleanse it—ensure that the net is secure in order to avoid it becoming loose and the skull falling out.
- place within an ancient stone circle or close to a standing stone—spending time in these sacred places will be beneficial to you, too.
- wrap in silk or another natural fiber—you could also make a bag out of the material, and place the skull in it when you take it anywhere with you.
- stroke with a feather—traditionally this should be an eagle feather, but it is very unlikely that you will have one of these, therefore, any feather that you find, while outdoors, will work well.

** not suitable for amethyst and fluorite as the sun will fade the colors of these minerals.

The following methods are only for skulls carved from minerals with a hardness number of 7 or above:

- leave outside in the rain—only suitable, if you are sure that it is not acid rain that is falling.
- place in the sea, a lake, a river, or a stream—keep a close eye on the skull, if it is quite small, because the movement of water, particularly that of the tide, can take the skull out beyond your reach.
- place in a solution of spring water and 2 drops of the Bach Flower Remedy Crab Apple—the essence of the crab apple tree is very cleansing.
- in addition, add 4 drops of Bach Rescue Remedy—if you believe the skull has been traumatized in some way.
- place in a solution of spring water and essential oil(s),

e.g. Juniper, Rosemary, Lemon—these are considered cleansing, but if you have other essential oil preferences, use those instead.
- hold under running water or place in sea salt water—hold the skull firmly while it is under the running water, so that it does not slip out of your hand.

Using Other Methods:

- trace sacred symbols on its surface, or place in/on a geometric pattern—symbols can be traced with your finger directly onto the skull. Draw the geometric shape on paper with pen or pencil.
- give healing to it—e.g. Reiki, but if you are not a 'hands-on' healer, hold the skull and mentally send it loving thoughts.
- place inside a pyramid—the metal frame type of pyramid, but if by any chance you are visiting the pyramids in Egypt or Mexico, then most definitely take the skull with you.
- rotate a pendulum clockwise over it—particularly effective if the pendulum is made from a crystal.
- give loving gestures—e.g. kisses, cuddles, or gentle strokes.
- pass through the smoke of burning incense or smudge sticks—I have found that smudging works very well on amethyst.
- pass through a candle flame—be careful not to burn your fingers.
- place on an altar, a shrine, or within a sacred space—you can designate an area within your home as a sacred space by bringing into it candles, incense, a water fountain, crystals, a Buddha, a Goddess ornament, a Menorah, a Madonna, or any spiritual effigy that is meaningful to you.

- visualize Divine Light passing through it—imagine this as being golden, or white, or a rainbow of colors.
- visualize holding it under a Divine waterfall—if you imagine that you are also standing under the waterfall while holding the skull, you will receive healing, as well.
- visualize different colors passing through it—blue and green are considered healing colors, but use whichever ones you feel are appropriate.

Depending on how much your crystal skull has been misused, traumatized, or filled with negative energy, one cleansing treatment may not be sufficient. There are no set rules with regards how long and how often a mineral specimen needs to be cleansed. When you work closely with the mineral kingdom, you will acquire a sense of the extent of negativity within your crystal skull, as well as an awareness of when it is completely removed. You will also know when it has picked up negative energy, again. In the beginning, however, it is best to remember my guidelines on how minerals can become 'dirty,' and to cleanse them whenever you know they have been exposed to one or more of those ways. Try to do this as soon as possible, especially if you intend using your crystal skull within a healing or therapeutic session. I believe healers and therapists have a responsibility to ensure that they do not use uncleansed crystal tools while working with a client. This means cleansing your crystal skull immediately after one client has left and before the next client arrives.

Whereas cleansing will be an ongoing process throughout the time the crystal skull remains with you, dedication is a one-time procedure. I learned how to dedicate a mineral specimen while in training to become a crystal healing practitioner at the UK's International College of Crystal Healing. The concept of dedication is to ensure that, should your crystal skull fall into the hands of someone who would wish to misuse its properties, his/her attempts to do so will be thwarted. It is as though you are placing a shield of protection all around the skull. Within this procedure, you are dedicating the skull to the Divine and asking that it can only be used for the very highest good. Dedication is performed immediately after the original cleansing process, which takes place as soon as the crystal skull has arrived in your home. The following ritual is how I dedicate all of my crystal skulls and you are welcome to copy it. Having cleansed the skull in some manner, I sit holding it in my hands with my eyes closed. Then I say:

> "I dedicate this skull to Love, Light and the Highest Good, that the Oneness may come, again. I ask that it be used with only the very Highest, Finest and Purest intentions and that only the very Highest, Finest and Purest vibrations are allowed to pass through it. So be it, so be it, and so it is."

You can substitute your own words or even add a prayer for the dedication. Whatever feels comfortable and right for you, will work best.

The third and last thing you need to do with your crystal skull before beginning to work with it, is to tune it to whatever purpose you have in mind. Whether for scrying or healing, for your own spiritual development, or to learn its secrets, you are asking the skull to focus on your reason for acquiring it. Some people call this process "programming," but I am not happy with that word. To me it implies that I have power over the skull, if I program it to do the work I want from it. Even tuning suggests that I have some of the control over what will happen, but it feels more appropriate to me. Basically, when I tune any mineral, I am stating the work with which I need help, and I am asking for its assistance. I always add that I should only be given this help, if what I want is right and appropriate for me.

Minerals can be tuned and retuned as frequently as required. They can also be tuned to more than one need at the same time. So ask for your crystal skull's help and it will be given. If you purchased the skull with no specific reason for acquiring it in mind, just ask it to work with you in whatever manner is best for your soul's development.

Chapter Twelve

THE RESPONSIBILITY OF BEING A CRYSTAL SKULL CUSTODIAN

Your crystal skull will work with you in whatever capacity you have asked of it and, I believe, it is your responsibility to take care of it in a loving and respectful manner. Deciding where to keep it may pose a problem. It needs to be somewhere that is safe from any kind of damage, where it cannot be dropped, knocked over, or chipped. Dust is also a problem because its removal can cause scratches on the surface of the skull. The most common mineral to be found across this planet is quartz, and this means there is always a large quantity of it within dust. Therefore, dust has a hardness level of 7 and, as you remove it with a cloth, there is the possibility of scratching any mineral specimen that has a hardness level of 7 or less. Whenever possible, remove the dust by blowing it away or vacuuming the skull with a soft brush attachment. Alternatively, if your skull is made from a mineral that has a hardness of 7 or above, then you can rinse it under a faucet to wash away the dust.

Keeping your skull in a glass case or china cabinet will lessen the need for dusting. However, in my opinion and that of some other crystal skull custodians, many of them dislike being closed off from what is happening in your home. You will quickly become aware, if your crystal skull is not happy being behind glass. Depending on how 'in tune' with it you are, you may even hear it yelling at you to bring it out. Then it will make you aware of where it wants to be.

Perhaps, in your mind, you have the perfect place to put your skull. Once cleansed, dedicated and tuned, you position it there and you are well pleased with your choice of location. Yet this may not be where the crystal skull wants to be, and it will pester you to be removed. You may have to make several attempts at finding the right place before the correct one is established. Allow yourself to be open to any thoughts, ideas and impressions that come to you unexpectedly with regards its placement. These are not actually coming from you, but are your crystal skull communicating with you.

You may be given the impression that your crystal skull wants to go with you when you are on vacation or visiting another place. Toltelcul accompanied my husband and me when we were in Glastonbury for a week in July 1999. While staying in our hotel, which was once a coaching inn dating back some five hundred years, he sat on one of the window-sills in our room. The windows looked down onto the main street of the town and there was always plenty of activity below. When we visited the Tor, the Abbey ruins and the Chalice Well Gardens, Toltelcul was with us. I placed him in the Red Spring water that runs through the Gardens and, I believe, that has given him an additional healing quality.

If you take your crystal skull out and about, make sure it is wrapped in bubble wrap, or plenty of tissue paper, or some type of cloth, so that it will not be damaged in transit. If you bring it out to enjoy the energies of certain places, such as, a stone circle or at the beach, remember to carefully pack it away, again, before leaving. Watch over it as you would anything or anyone that is precious to you. Your skull friend will appreciate the care you provide for it and will give back many blessings.

Some people do not like others to touch or pick up their crystals. This is one method of protecting their mineral specimens from the possibility of taking on negative energy. You may feel this way about your crystal skull, and you have a right to ask people to only look and not touch. I, however, have never prevented people from handling my crystals and crystal skulls. I know that when they hold them, they are gaining some benefit from the contact. There are no right or wrong theories about this matter, there is only the need to identify your feelings and to act upon them. You may also want to think about how you can best protect your crystal friend from being stolen, whether it is in your home or accompanying you as you go out and about. If the skull should fall into the wrong hands, it may be misused or treated with disrespect.

Apart from recognizing your responsibility with regards the proper care of your skull, there are two further obligations that need consideration. A crystal skull is a very powerful tool whose properties function on the subtle levels, as well as on the physical plane. Do not use this power indiscriminately or with anything other than the very highest of objectives. Misuse and/or neglect of your crystal friend will probably lead to difficulties and setbacks within your personal life. Your inappropriate actions and thoughts will also set in motion the law of karma. Remember the saying, "What goes around, comes around!" This is most definitely true when working with the mineral kingdom. Therefore, handle your crystal skull with respect and loving care in the same way as you would want to be treated yourself.

The last commitment that becomes yours when you acquire a crystal skull, is not to allow this powerful mineral carving to affect people in any way other than what is conducive to their spiritual development. When you begin to bring crystals, crystal skulls and mineral specimens into any area, the energy vibrations within that place are changed. Some people are far more sensitive and less protected on the subtle levels than others, and their auric energies can be greatly affected when they are in the presence of members of the mineral kingdom. The higher vibrations of crystals can cause a person's subtle energy to become unbalanced as it attempts to emulate that lofty pattern. What affects the subtle anatomy/aura is reflected down to the physical body, and these people may experience headaches, nausea, or feel light-headed. It is also possible for them to feel mental confusion and emotional disturbances. Put simply, they have become ungrounded by the mineral's accelerated energy vibration. Therefore, you will need to ask your crystal skull to attune itself to the energy vibration of each and every adult and child who comes into the area where it is located. This may be your home, your therapy room, or your office, wherever the crystal skull is being kept. Ask that it affects each person to a level that is appropriate for him/her and in a manner that is right for soul development. You do not have to begin naming people because you are making this request for all persons who will come within the skull's proximity. This may even include someone making a delivery to your home or therapy room. Request this of your crystal skull as soon as you have cleansed, dedicated and tuned it and ask that it continues to do this indefinitely. Remember to make the same request each time you add to your collection of crystal skulls. You can make a similar plea on behalf of any animals and pets that are living in or visiting the place where your crystal skull is housed.

I have followed this practice for many years. Long before

I began to collect crystal skulls, I was aware that many people, who came into my home, were being affected by my crystals. I made a one-time request, similar to my suggestion above, of all my existing crystals and then asked the same of each new one as it arrived. I have continued to make this request of each crystal skull, too. It is fascinating for me to see how well this system works. Some people can be in my home for many hours and are oblivious of my many crystals and mineral carvings. Others will see them or remark about the special crystal energy they can feel, even as they enter my home.

When you have completed all of the recommendations and responsibilities that I have previously explained, you are ready to begin working closely with your crystal friend. Apart from the various requests that you may have made of this skull, there are other processes and exercises that you can pursue together. Some of these are detailed in the following pages. Also, remember to be accepting of any other experiences and information sharing that are initiated by your crystal skull. In this way your life will most definitely change and become more purposeful. You have become the custodian of an amazing and powerful, spiritual ally.

PART THREE

Working With Your Crystal Skull

Chapter Thirteen

SELF-HEALING, SELF-PROTECTION, MEDITATION & DREAMWORK

It is said that the mineral kingdom helps us with grief, but I would go further and say that it is helpful with all our emotions, our physical ailments, our mental attitudes and our spiritual development. If you have a crystal skull, you are equipped with a powerful tool for self-healing. However, at this point I would like to state that healing and medicine are two entirely different fields. Therefore, any healing exercises given in this and the following chapter should not be looked upon as being, or in place of, medical advice. I would always recommend consulting a medical practitioner when experiencing sickness.

If you know you have a specific illness of the physical, the emotional, the mental, or even the spiritual level, then you can ask your crystal skull to work with you on this problem.

However, sickness may manifest at one of these levels, but, in fact, it may have begun on a different level. We are often unaware of the source of our dis-eases and, if this source is left untreated, disharmony can prevail throughout all levels of being.

The mineral kingdom has a wonderful ability to pinpoint and treat the source of any dis-ease and disharmony, no matter at what level they may manifest. This is what sets crystal healing apart from many other therapies. Therefore, you do not need to know at what level your illness became a reality. Merely allow the mineral kingdom to work with you in a healing capacity, and your crystal skull will seek out and help to heal the cause of your dis-ease.

The following exercises will promote self-healing and they should take place where there will be no interruptions. If you have pets, be aware that they may try to join you. Cats and dogs are sensitive to the energy vibration of healing sessions and meditations and they want to experience what is happening. If you know your pet will remain quiet within the room where you are holding a self-healing session, then allow it to be with you. At the beginning of each exercise, sit in a high-back chair or on the floor, resting your back against a wall. In order to anchor the healing energy well into your physical body, remove your shoes and place the soles of your feet on the floor. This is one method of grounding energy. Make sure your ankles or legs are not crossed because this will cause a blockage to the energy flow. If you should drift into sleep during a session, this will not interfere with the healing process.

Once you feel sure you are sitting comfortably, close your eyes and center yourself by imagining you are entering the very core of your whole being. Do this in whatever way is appropriate for you, accepting any images or impressions that are given to you. Next, begin taking full, deep breaths, doing so in your own time and at your own pace. With each out-breath, know that you are becoming more and more relaxed. At this point, ask for Divine protection throughout the exercise and that the healing, which you are about to receive, is only to the extent that is right and appropriate for you at this time. Also, request that it is given at whatever level or levels it is needed. During each of the following exercises, you should remain sitting quietly with eyes closed for at least fifteen minutes. At the end of each session, thank the crystal skull or skulls that have participated in the healing and remember to thoroughly cleanse it or them.

At different times and, if possible, try each of the four self-healing exercises listed below. Then decide which one works best for you and hold a session whenever you feel the need for healing. It is not necessary to have specific types of crystal properties in order for these exercises to work, therefore, you can use skulls that have been carved from any mineral.

Self-Healing Exercise One:

Before beginning this session, place your crystal skull somewhere close at hand. Once you have completed your grounding, centering and deep, relaxing breathing, make your request for protection. Next, pick up the skull, holding it with both hands and resting it on your lap. Be sure it is right-side-up and facing you. Ask for the healing to begin. Now, sit still and enjoy whatever sensations, visions, and experiences may come to you during this time. They are all part of the healing process.

Self-Healing Exercise Two:

As with the above exercise, sit holding your crystal skull in exactly the same manner. With eyes remaining closed, visualize a vibrant green light radiating from every part of the skull. This healing color moves into your hands, along your arms, then travels throughout your whole body. It reaches from the top of your head right down to your toes. Allow this green, healing light to remain with you for several minutes, then gently let it fade. Next, visualize an intense blue light radiating from every part of the skull and this, in turn, spreads throughout your body. Again, hold onto a sense of this healing color being within you for a while. Finally, allow its intensity to dissipate.

If several crystal skulls are in your keeping, then the following two exercises will be possible to do.

Self-Healing Exercise Three:

Prior to beginning your deep breathing, be sure that you have two crystal skulls of similar size close by. These skulls do not have to be carved from the same type of mineral. When fully relaxed, place one skull in your left hand and the other in your right hand. If you are right-handed, the skull in that hand should be facing away from you and the one in your left hand should be facing you. If you are left-handed, then hold the skulls in the reverse manner from the one just explained. Make your request for protection and healing. During this exercise, healing energy will enter your body via the inward-facing skull. It will travel into your hand, up your arm and throughout your entire body. If there is any dis-ease or disharmony within you, it will then be pushed towards, and exit via, the outward-facing skull. Sit quietly until you feel the process has been completed.

Self-Healing Exercise Four:

With the aid of a compass, establish the four directions (North, South, East and West) within the room where the session will take place. Next, beginning in the East and moving clockwise, place one crystal skull on the floor in each of these four directions, but facing into the center of the room. Each skull should be similar in size to the other three and can be fashioned from a different mineral or all four can be of the same type. You can also use a combination of two minerals that are the same with two others that are the same as each other. Allow sufficient space in the middle of these crystal skulls for you to either sit down on the floor or on a chair placed in the center of them. Be sure you are facing East. Begin your deep breathing to help you relax and, once again, ask for protection and healing. Remain seated while the healing takes place. When we place ourselves in the center of the four directions and ask for healing, we retrieve all our scattered energies together with any parts of our essence that have been fragmented. The presence of the crystal skulls within those four directions greatly enhances and focuses the process.

* * *

When we meditate, give or receive healing, channel and work in any capacity at the inner levels of existence, we open up all of our subtle bodies. This then means we can become vulnerable to a whole range of energies, some of which may not be of a positive nature. Therefore, it is important to learn how to protect ourselves at these levels during our waking and sleeping hours. With this in mind, I am including two exercises for self-protection.

As with the healing exercises, you will need to find a quiet place where you can relax and pursue the exercises without being disturbed. You may also wish to conduct one of them immediately prior to commencing a self-healing session or any of the other exercises that are discussed in this or the next chapter. Do not forget to ground and center yourself, when you begin, or to thank and cleanse the crystal skulls that participate in these exercises, when you are finished.

Self-Protection Exercise One:

For preference, use a clear quartz skull for this exercise. Once your deep breathing has completely relaxed you, sit holding your crystal skull with it facing towards you. Visualize the color purple emanating from it and spreading all around you. Breathe in this color and be aware that it not only fills every part of your physical body, but also moves into all of your subtle bodies, filling them with its vibration of protection. Continue to experience this process for fifteen to twenty minutes.

Self-Protection Exercise Two:

This exercise will work best if you use skulls that have been carved from amethyst, obsidian, smoky quartz, or red jasper. These are considered to be very protective minerals. You can use any combination of these four minerals. Place four crystal skulls of similar size in the four directions and facing outwards. As with Self-Healing Exercise Four, begin in the East and move in a clockwise motion. Sit in the center of these skulls, facing East and, once you are relaxed, ask that you be given protection from any evil coming from the East, the South, the West and the North, at all times and on all levels of your being. Remain seated and receive the protective energies for fifteen to twenty minutes.

Exercises for self-protection should be conducted on a regular basis, especially if you are a healer, a therapist, a medium, or anyone who is working in a metaphysical capacity.

* * *

The mineral kingdom is extremely helpful within meditation. What you experience during this quiet time will be enhanced threefold, if crystal skulls lend their aid to the process. You will also learn much about your crystal friend, if you meditate with it. As explained in Chapter Seven, it is one form of communication between the two of you. If you are not accustomed to meditating, then I would suggest you become familiar with practicing it before including any mineral in a meditation session. It takes time and repeated effort to learn how to quiet the conscious mind and allow the inner you to reveal itself. Meditation should be pursued regularly and with dedication. It is a discipline. Once it has become a part of your life, try the following exercises.

Meditation Exercise One:

Sit in a high-back chair or on the floor with a crystal skull close by you. Breathe deeply to help you relax. At this point, ground and center yourself and ask for Divine protection throughout the exercise. This is important because during meditation you are opening up at many levels. Still your mind, pick up the crystal skull and hold it facing towards you. Now, ask to be given whatever is appropriate for your spiritual development at this time. During subsequent sessions, you can ask for information about the skull itself or anything that is of interest to you. Meditation times will vary from person to person, but they usually remain constant with the amount of time to which you are accustomed. When this exercise has ended, thank and cleanse the crystal skull. As a variation of this exercise and particularly if your crystal skull is heavy, position it in front of you and place both hands over it during the meditation. If you are sitting on a chair, it could be put on a table in front of you.

Meditation Exercise Two:

You will need two crystal skulls of similar size and preferably of the same mineral for this exercise. Sit on the floor in the middle of the room and place a skull, facing inwards, on either side of you. Each one should be at least twelve inches away from you. Relax, ground and center yourself, then ask for Divine protection. Now, with the power of your mind imagine that an energy vibration builds from each crystal skull and forms an archway over you. This energy structure then extends down in front of and behind you until you are completely within its safe and sacred space. Think of this as being a meditation dome, and ask to be given spiritual guidance. When you have finished meditating and before you stand up, imagine the structure of this dome retracting back completely into the crystal skulls. As always, give your thanks and a cleansing to both skulls.

Meditation Exercise Three:

If you are the custodian of a large, clear quartz skull, you may feel the need to be a part of the upgrading of our planet and the Universal Light Gridwork. If this is so, I would suggest that you sit quietly in meditation with your skull and ask to be shown how you can best support this divine reformation. You may be told specific actions to take with your clear quartz companion, or entirely different functions may be requested of you. Whatever is asked of you, do these things with reverence and love, and know that you are one of many Light workers existing across this planet.

Meditation sessions that are enhanced by minerals usually give vivid images, clear messages and strong impressions. What is given during these times is also less nebulous, being easier to recall and with greater accuracy.

* * *

As Chapter Seven illustrated, crystal skulls can give information within your dreams. If you are interested in experiencing how they can do this when you sleep, either take one to bed with you or place one on your bedside table. It is more comfortable to take a small skull, which you can place under your pillow or hold in your hand, into the bed. A larger skull should be put on the bedside table. However, this is also a suitable place for a small skull. When choosing the bedside table option, be certain that the crystal skull is within a three foot radius of your body. This will ensure that it is in your auric space and, therefore, will optimize the mineral's impact upon your dreams.

Before going to bed, there are a couple of things you may wish to do. If the floor of your bedroom is not carpeted, place a towel or cloth on the floor near to the bed. It is possible for the crystal skull to be pushed out of the bed when you move around in your sleep. This will help lessen the impact of the fall and avoid breakage. If you are interested in documenting your dreams, have a notepad and a pen close at hand before you go to sleep. As soon as you are awake, you can record what you have experienced.

Once you are in bed, ask to remain well grounded, centered and protected throughout the night, and then make a request of the crystal skull. There may be some specific information that you want to receive while you are sleeping, or you can just ask it to oversee your dreams. With either choice, be sure to state that you wish to be given only what is right and appropriate for you at this time. If someone else is in the bed with you, also ask the crystal skull to not affect him/her during the hours of sleep. This will make sure that you are not imposing your will over another person's will. Now, go to sleep and enjoy your dreams.

On waking, remember to thank your crystal skull and cleanse it, once you are up and about. If more than one crystal skull is in your keeping, try taking a different one to bed on another night.

Chapter Fourteen

HEALING & PROTECTION EXERCISES FOR OTHERS

Before explaining how to conduct distant healing and protection-for-another exercises, I want to state that, I believe, it is important to gain permission from the intended recipient before commencing. When you do this, you are acknowledging that there is always free will, as well as demonstrating your respect of this concept. If someone seeks your service for himself/herself, then you obviously have the required permission. However, there may be occasions when people ask you to perform these exercises for someone else. Before doing so, you should ensure that consent for them to make this request has been given. There may also be times when this will not be possible. For example, when sending distant healing to an adult who is comatose, or to a small child, or to an animal, you will not be able to gain the recipient's agreement. In these instances, seek permission from the closest relative, the parents, or the pet owners.

Even if these individuals give their consent, I suggest you also gain permission from the Higher Self of the adult, the child, or the animal. For any life form within the animal kingdom, including humans, this is the part of the soul that watches over and guides the physical aspect of the soul. Acquiring this permission can be done quite easily in the following manner: Sit quietly, allowing yourself to relax. Next, ask to be brought into the presence of the Higher Self of the individual in question. Once you are made aware in some manner of this aspect of the person, child, or animal, make your request for permission to send distant healing and/or protection. If it is granted, you can proceed with the exercise. If it is not, do not go against the wishes of the Higher Self.

In all circumstances where you will be offering this service, agree upon a day and time with the recipient, the relatives, or the pet owners, for the exercise to take place. This is particularly helpful for any recipient who is not confined in some manner and is living a normal, active life. These exercises can impact strongly on them, therefore, they should not be engaged in some form of activity while the process is taking place. I have heard horror stories about people, who did not know someone was sending them distant healing, suddenly feeling dizzy or disorientated while driving a car or doing something that required their concentration and alertness.

If possible, when arranging the time of the exercise, ask that the recipient remains seated and relaxed for whatever length of time you intend to send healing or protection. With regards an animal, the owners may be able to encourage their pet to sit or lie down. For a child, naptime or bedtime is an ideal situation. When the people, who have requested distant healing or protection, live in different time zones from yours, you may be able to conduct the exercises while they are asleep. This appears to be a particularly beneficial time to receive these energies. I have been given feedback from a number of individuals who experienced extremely pleasant dreams during the time I was pursuing these exercises for them.

With these and any other type of exercises that are explained in this book, lighting a candle and burning incense at the beginning will prove helpful. As always, be sure you are well-grounded, centered and protected before commencing. Also, use deep breathing to become relaxed, and at the end make sure you have thanked and cleansed any crystal skulls that have participated.

Distant Healing Exercise One:

Have a crystal skull close at hand when you sit on the floor or in a high-back chair. Once you are fully relaxed, pick up the skull and hold it with both hands and facing away from you. Ask the skull to send healing energy to the individual for whom you are conducting the session. Make this request for all levels of the recipient's being and to the extent that is right and appropriate at this time. If you are a Reiki Level II or III practitioner, send the Cho-Ku-Rei symbol along with your request in order to boost the power of the healing. Sending loving thoughts to the person, child, or animal will create a similar effect, if you have not been attuned to Reiki. Remain seated for at least fifteen minutes and repeat the process twice more on other days.

Distant Healing Exercise Two:

Proceed as above in Exercise One, but imagine that you are placing the Cho-Ku-Rei or the loving thoughts within the crystal skull. You may wish to trace the Reiki symbol over the cranium of the skull as a way of emphasizing this. If you are familiar with this person, child, or animal, summon up a mental image of him/her in front of you. If you are not acquainted with the recipient, ask to be given an impression of him/her. Next, visualize yourself handing the crystal skull to the recipient of the distant healing and, with the power of your imagination, see this individual holding the skull and receiving healing energy from it. If the recipient is a small child or animal, visualize yourself placing the crystal skull beside him/her, and know that healing is taking place. Hold onto either image for several minutes, and then let it slowly fade. Repeat this exercise on two other days.

* * *

There are occasions when people ask me to conduct protection exercises for them. This usually happens when they believe they are under psychic attack from someone or something. Similarly, others may be prompted to make this request of you. There may also be times when you feel a family member or friend is in need of protection. If the latter is true, remember to gain permission before commencing. Both of the following exercises can also be pursued for a child or any animal that appears to be in need of protection. Whatever the situation may be, crystal skulls can greatly enhance protective energy.

Protection-For-Another Exercise One:

Place four crystal skulls on the floor or on a table and have them facing outwards to the four directions. If possible, use amethyst, obsidian, smoky quartz, or red jasper skulls in any combination that is available to you. Leave sufficient space in the center of the skulls to place a "witness" of the person, child, or animal for whom you are conducting the exercise. This can be a photograph, a lock of hair, or some item that belongs to him or her. Sit close to the layout of crystal skulls and witness and begin your deep breathing to relax yourself. Now, request that protection is given at all times and on all levels of the recipient's being. Ask that all evil coming from the East be guarded against, then repeat this requirement for the South, for the West and for the North. Sit quietly, concentrating on your request, for at least fifteen minutes before ending the session. Leave the layout in place for as long as possible. Preferably, do not remove the crystal skulls and witness until either the recipient believes, or you are certain, there is no further need for protection. At this time, your thanks and a crystal skulls' cleansing will be appropriate.

Protection-For-Another Exercise Two:

If you are not a Reiki Level II or III practitioner and prior to beginning this exercise, sit quietly, relax and ask to be shown a symbol that brings protection. No matter what design, image, or object is given to you, know that it is yours to use for protection. Now, follow the procedure for Distant Healing Exercise Two, but imagine you are placing the protective symbol that you were given inside the skull. If you know the Reiki symbols, then the powerful Sei-He-Ki is the one to use. As previously suggested, you can trace either symbol onto the skull's cranium. Next, within your mind see yourself handing the crystal skull to the person or placing it beside the child or animal, and be aware that they are now well protected. Hold onto this visualization for as long as possible. The image will be more distinct if you know the recipient, but the process will work, even if you do not. End the session only after the image has completely faded from your mind. Give thanks and cleanse the crystal skull.

I have been a practitioner of Crystal Healing and Reiki for a number of years. I have also held sessions for sending distant healing and protection for the same amount of time.

As previously mentioned in Chapter Three, if I compare the results of the hands-on procedures with those that were conducted from a distance, the latter have proved to be more powerful and successful. Therefore, if you choose to pursue any of the exercises given in this chapter, be aware that you are working with an energy force that is extremely strong. Please use it with respect, sincerity and gratitude.

Epilogue

I believe minerals are the life-blood of our planet and, therefore, are equally essential to our very existence. In addition, they have proved themselves to be tools for healing and spirituality. Having worked closely for a number of years with crystals and minerals, I am convinced they have properties that defy everyday explanation. My more recent explorations with crystal skulls have only added to my admiration for the mineral kingdom. However, I am also left with some puzzling thoughts and questions about both these carvings and the human skull. In these final words of this book I do not profess to have the answers, I merely put forward my own ruminations on these matters, as well as some answers that I have been given by my angelic guides.

What is it that sets crystal skulls apart from any other carved and polished mineral specimens? People who collect crystals, gemstones and minerals, experience a bonding with them, but the attachment to crystal skulls is much more profound. Could there be a very simple answer about why this happens? Do we feel an affinity with them because, at a subconscious level, we realize they mirror our inward physical appearance? Or is the reason more complex? The ancients believed the soul resided in the skull, therefore, this part of human anatomy was revered. Was this a primeval misunderstanding or sacred knowledge that became lost over time? In very early infancy we recognize others by smell and sound. Yet once vision becomes focused, we smile at another person's face, not at his/her hand, or shoulder, or back. Does this mean that there is something deeply entrenched within us about the human skull? Or is it merely the fact that an infant's first and repeated clear view of its world is the profile of its mother's face, as it suckles at the breast?

As I have previously explained, in June and July of 1999 the Voladi told me that crystal skulls are a communication tool between humans and other beings. In Chapter Four I gave the beginning of a message from them in which they spoke about certain, ancient crystal skulls. The remaining passage follows and perhaps it tells us why we feel so close to these carvings:

"... But we wish you to understand that crystal skulls are not just communication or even healing devices, they are a form of the Divine, as are we all. Human hands have fashioned many of them, and the human individual would be imprinting into the skull the closeness that exists between the animal kingdom and the mineral kingdom, as the creation of the skull took place. This knowledge is held within the DNA of humans and other animals, and for most it is not a conscious knowledge. As the skull takes shape, Divine consciousness recognizes Divine consciousness and the bond is sealed. For the mineral specimen, this is a complete and lasting understanding, but for the human, it is often unrealized or dismissed as a fanciful thought. This recognition does not only take place when minerals are being fashioned into various shapes, such as, skulls. Once a member of the mineral kingdom and one of the animal kingdom come into the proximity of each other, the link is established. This will help you to understand why some individuals believe a crystal or mineral specimen chose them rather than they made the conscious choice to acquire it.

The mineral fashioned into a skull shape is in actuality a simple yet profound, coded message for humans: "We are very alike despite our dissimilarities. We are both expressions of the Divine One."

Furthermore, if we can accept that crystal skulls are tools for communication between sentient beings, existing in different dimensions, then it would follow that they also connect the various levels of existence with each other. In a recently channeled message, I was told how this became possible. It is an intriguing concept and I offer it here for your consideration, but first I need to give some lead-in, background information on it.

In one of the chapters of my book *Soul Wisdom, Volume One*, I explain about the seeding of man on Earth. This information was given to me in 1985 by one of my angelic guides. There are details in that chapter about Watchers who came from Orion in order to monitor the development of man. There is also a description in the book of a vision I had in February 1986, during meditation, in which I saw my angelic guide, named Moon, as a Watcher. Below is an extract from that description:

> "... When I first saw him, I thought he had horns, but then I could see that he was wearing some kind of headgear or band around his head. The two ends of this headgear went up into the air above the front of his head, giving the impression of horns. The section around the head was a luminous, white color, but the part above the head was dark ... " [1]

Over the years, I have never given much thought as to what this headgear might have been, but, as is shown further below, Moon has finally explained.

The Orion Watchers brought with them five devices that contained all knowledge. These devices were to be left with man so that he could eventually learn their secrets. The role of the Watchers was to keep their vigil and not interfere with man's progression. However, certain Watchers began to share their knowledge with the early man forms, long before it was appropriate for them to do so. Consequently, only three of the devices were left on our planet. One was kept on the land mass in the Pacific known to some as Mu, the second was placed on Atlantis and the third was secreted in the Caucasus mountains. At the present time, all three devices are lost to us. The one on Mu sank beneath the ocean with that continent, and the second was brought by Thoth from Atlantis to Egypt and buried beneath the Great Pyramid. The third lies underground, deep within present-day Palestine, after it had at one time been kept in the Ark of the Covenant.

Both I and my older son asked several questions about these devices at the time the information was given, but we were only told they were of a technology that our modern civilization has not pursued. However, within a channeled reading for a man in the US in November 1998, there was mention of a link between the technology of the devices and the work of Dr. Nikola Tesla with regards to The Philadelphia Experiment. If you are not familiar with this subject, I suggest you search the Internet for it. It is one of many covert operations and incidents that have never been fully or truthfully shared with the general public. More recently, while writing this book, I have been receiving impressions that these devices were connected to crystal skulls in some manner. Therefore, during an automatic writing session, I asked my angelic guide about this connection. His explanation began as follows:

> "In order to give you an answer to your question, I must first put forward an understanding of the mineral kingdom. As you have become aware, minerals are but one of many facets of the Source. They are as much a part of our progenitor as are we. They have, however, maintained a powerful and lucid link with their other levels of existence. Unlike many other life forms that reside on planets within the physical universe, minerals in the physical are completely in harmony with their beingness throughout the Spiral. Thus, you will comprehend why they hold infinite knowledge of WHAT IS . . ."

Due to this strong link that they possess with the other aspects of themselves, it was decided that a mineral should form the basis of the Watchers' devices. By this means, there could be two-way communication and information sharing between the physical mineral device and a particular, spirit level of that same mineral. Moon continued:

> " . . . The device was constructed from a mineral on Pleteris (a planet within the Orion Constellation) that is similar to Earth's quartz, but a section of it was infused with its counterpart in (archangel) Michael's level. When you saw an image of me as I appeared to Toa, I was wearing the device around my head. What appeared to you as horns, were the anchors that kept the device within the physical, and the luminous section was a combination of the mineral's physical and Michael's level attributes. When not in use, the device could be carried as you observed, but when needed, it was turned around and placed so that the protruding pieces faced downwards at the back of the head and the luminous section encircled the brow

and most of the cranium. Once in place, a crystalline mask would descend from the luminous section and form over the brow chakra, the eyes, and also across the cranium. Information would then be imparted from Michael's level to the physical brain of the one using this instrument of learning. At the same time, what was being experienced within physical existence was being given to the mineral's counterpart at Michael's level so that he and his companions could then access it. When the information sharing was completed, the mask retracted back into the luminous section. Please understand that I created an instrument for two-way communication and knowledge sharing. Also, know that the Watchers' device was highly volatile and could only be used safely by those who, like me, did not fully project into physical form . . . "

Many of the Watchers from Pleteris did not fully become a part of physical existence. They preferred to dip in and out of their earthly forms.

When certain Watchers began prematurely sharing ancient wisdoms with early man, it was decided to abandon usage of the devices. An alternative method of disseminating knowledge was created by the archangel Michael. The following is the remainder of the channeled message about the connection between the Watchers' devices and crystal skulls, and it would appear to explain why the latter are such remarkable objects:

". . . Michael put forward an alternative method of exchanging information between his level and the physical plane. He wanted it to be one that would gradually teach man about WHAT IS, but also to be a means by which man could access the knowledge himself without the aid of Watchers and their devices.

Michael reasoned that because Watchers on Pleteris and Earth often took the form of what could be considered man, those who used the device placed it upon their heads rather than any other part of their bodies. It then followed that the minerals existing at his level would easily recognize, and find conducive to their needs, the skull shape. Michael concluded that the inherent linking of minerals between his level and the physical plane could be accelerated, if the physical mineral took on the form of a human skull. This could then mean the two-way connection between his level and the earth plane would be available to man in a more stable, less harmful and much slower manner than the functioning of the Watchers devices.

With the magick of his realms, he fashioned one life-size skull from a block of earthly, clear quartz. He instructed the minerals existing at his level to exchange information with this mineral skull more rapidly than their usual connection with physical minerals, which had not been shaped thus. Michael knew that once this original and quicker method of linking was established, it would then hold true for any other physical minerals that took on the form of a skull.

Eventually, two other mineral skulls were fashioned by means of Michael's magick, and the three were placed across your planet. These three then gave ancient man much of the technology that sprang from crystalline energy. With the further passage of physical time, more mineral skulls were created by means of this crystalline energy, and the three original skulls departed from the earth plane. They returned to Michael's level where they continue to exist. With the eventual loss of the knowledge of crystalline energy, mineral skulls were ultimately fashioned by physical carving. Many forgot the true purpose of mineral skulls and used them in other ways, yet each retains the ability to allow man to access the knowledge of WHAT IS.

Now, you will understand why all skulls, which have been carved from minerals at any time, link to WHAT IS..."

As I was given this information quite recently, I have not yet asked any follow-up questions of Moon. However, on completion of this book, I intend to do so.

The other aspect of crystal skulls that thoroughly intrigues me is their close link with change. Everyone that I interviewed corroborated my own findings about a crystal skull's ability to herald transformation and to assist while it is happening. In my experience, this premise does not necessarily hold true for minerals, therefore, why does this happen? I can only conclude that the skull shape has some hidden property that creates this phenomenon. The skull itself is often portrayed as a symbol of death, which is definitely an expression of change. Yet the differences and variations in the course of a person's life that accompany the acquisition of a crystal skull are even more dynamic. It is as though, at the soul level, this mineral carving reminds us of our spiritual agenda, our dharma. By this I mean the soul agreements we make prior to a physical existence. We set ourselves lessons to learn, deeds to do and relationships to procure, but once incarnated, we often forget to pursue our soul's plan-of-action. We stray from our spiritual progression and become embroiled in matters of the physical. Yet, when a crystal skull comes into our keeping, we are prompted to remember, at a deeper level, why we are here. The onset of the change may be quite drastic, as with my experience of Transverse Myelitis, but the ultimate outcome is always of benefit.

Writing this book has only deepened my interest in crystal skulls. I plan to do further research with my own mineral friends, as well as to continue networking with other crystal skull custodians. I am interested in conducting 'hands-on' healing sessions, using only these crystal carvings instead of other mineral specimens. As a crystal healing practitioner, I was taught to bring tumblestones, small clusters, crystal points, wands, spheres and rough stones into the healing space. I was also encouraged to discover my own, personal approach to crystal therapy and, I believe, the skulls will further develop this. I know that some people are incorporating color and sound into their work with crystal skulls, and I am hoping to explore these options, as well. In addition, with sixty-three crystal skulls presently in my and my husband's keeping, there will be plenty of opportunities to communicate and discover other sacred wisdoms through crystal skull meditations, dreamwork and channelings. I am particularly interested in working with a 15 lb. tigeriron skull, which recently arrived at our home. Named Adalan and displaying an androgynous energy signature, this new friend has hinted at having tales to tell about Atlantis.

In conclusion and if I have whet your appetite for a startling and mystical adventure, I suggest you step aside from your day-to-day life for a while and become the custodian of a crystal skull. I cannot tell you the exact details of what you will experience, but I can guarantee your life will take on greater meaning because you will have gained a spiritual and healing friend. And I invite you to share your adventure with me. My love and curiosity about these mineral carvings is never ending, and I am always interested in hearing more stories about them.

Love & Light
April 12, 2002
(New Moon in Aries)

1. Marion Webb-De Sisto, *Soul Wisdom, Volume One*, p. 131-132.

The Mohs Scale of Hardness for Minerals

1—Talc
2—Gypsum—e.g. Selenite, Alabaster.
3—Calcite
3.5—Azurite
4—Fluorite
4.5—Apophyllite
5—Apatite
5.5—Lazurite
6—Orthoclase Feldspar—e.g. Moonstone, Amazonite.
6.5—Opal
7—Quartz—e.g. Aventurine, Tigereye.
7.5—Beryl—e.g. Emerald, Aquamarine.
8—Topaz
9—Corundum—e.g. Sapphire, Ruby.
10—Diamond

Relevant Contact Details

People Featured In The Book:

Yolanda Badillo
Hairdresser/Astrologer/Homeopathy Consultant/Metaphysical
 Teacher
New York, NY., USA.
email: ybadillo@att.net

Sue Bouvier
Crystal Healing Practitioner/Spiritual Channel
Kent, UNITED KINGDOM.
email: suebou1@aol.com

Marc Edwards
Musician/Reiki Master
P.O. Box 1112
Midtown Station
New York, NY. 10018
USA.
email: marced@asan.com

Samantha 'Sam' Elliott
Reiki Master/Metaphysical Teacher
Eaton Bray, UNITED KINGDOM.
telephone: +44 (0) 1525 222131
email: sam@asuratherapy.co.uk
website: www.asuratherapy.co.uk

Frances Engelhardt
Yoga Teacher/Massage Therapist/Reiki Master/NLP Practitioner
'Gaia Visions Retreat'
36 Woodstock Avenue
Sutton, Surrey
SM3 9EF
UNITED KINGDOM.
telephone: +44 (0) 2084 018319
email: gaiavisions@yahoo.com
website: http://www.gaiavisions.co.uk

Fay Pohaikawahine Graef
Kukakuka (Dialogues) on things Hawaiian
California, USA.
email: efgraef45@aol.com

Linda
Reflexologist/Reiki Practitioner/Tarot Card Reader
London, UNITED KINGDOM.

Mark Loman
Goldsmith/Crystal Skull Collector & Enthusiast/Reiki Master/ Tarot Card Reader
'Gold Eye'
150 Huish
Yeovil, Somerset
BA20 1BN
UNITED KINGDOM.

telephone: +44 (0) 1935 478290
email: mark@yumyumi.freeserve.co.uk
website: http://www.goldeye.tsx.org

Kathleen Murray
Spiritual Channel/Metaphysical Lecturer
Galactic Publications (Earth)
PO BOX 11511
Huntly, Aberdeenshire
AB54 4WG
SCOTLAND
email: Skulls@crystal-keys.com
website: http://www.crystal-keys.com

Paula
Crystals/Minerals Collector & Enthusiast
The A-Z Medicinal Plants' Names Multi-Languages List
London, UNITED KINGDOM.
email: a-zmedicinalplantsnamesmulti-languageslist@care4free.net

Joshua 'Illinois' Shapiro
Crystal Skulls Researcher/Writer/Metaphysical Lecturer
'V J Enterprises'
9737 Fox Glen Dr. #1K
Niles, IL. 60714
USA.
telephone: (847)-824-1822
email: rjoshua@sprintmail.com
website: http://www.v-j-enterprises.com

C.'Ravenia' Todd
Crystal Skull Collector & Enthusiast/Animal Communicator
British Columbia, CANADA.
email: ravenia@thoughtandmemory.com

Raven H. Youngman
Master Skull Carver/Musician/Shaman
California, USA.
email: raven@ravensroost.net

Where To Buy Crystal Skulls:

(Wholesale Only)
'Raven's Roost'
607 W. Orangethorpe
Fullerton, CA. 92832
USA.
telephone: 714-526-6780
email: raven@ravensroost.net
website: http://www.ravensroost.net

(Wholesale Only)
Talisman Trading Company
Brazil.
email: talismanco@uol.com.br
website: http://www.talisman.com.br/tradco/ttcskull.html

(Retail)
'Thought and Memory'
2698 Nazko Road
Quesnel, British Columbia
V2J-7G5
CANADA.
email: ravenia@thoughtandmemory.com
website: http://www.thoughtandmemory.com

(Wholesale & Retail)
Burhouse Limited
Quarmby Mills
Tanyard Road

Oakes
Huddersfield, West Yorkshire
HD3 4YP.
UNITED KINGDOM.
telephone: +44 (0) 1484 655675
freephone: 0500 521522
fax: +44 (0) 1484 460036
email: sales@burhouse.demon.co.uk

Crystal Skulls Clubs & Groups:

http://groups.yahoo.com/group/crystalskullsclub

http://groups.yahoo.com/group/crystalskulls2

http://groups.yahoo.com/group/crystalskulls

http://www.crystalskullsociety.org/

Bibliography

Webb-De Sisto, Marion. *Soul Wisdom, Volume One*. Xlibris Corporation, 2000.

DNA realignment/attunement p52
p57 bk details - interesting
p60. The Divine Spark of Creation. The Crystal Skull Speaks
    s pages 73

p9 - energy vibration - ask to align crystal skull
p66. festival of Holistic living. hend on (August?)
p86. use skull rather than rock.

The Divine Spark of Creation: The Crystal Skull Speaks
Kathleen
Mysteries of the Crystal Skulls Revealed
Sandra Bowen, FR Nocerino & Joshua Shapiro
Journeys of a Crystal Skull Explorer - Joshua Shapiro p57

P96 Skull - for Museum. Human Image Exhibition
p 97 - new custodian
P39. attune to energy vibration of (Dad)
   P166 WHAT IS
P20 androgenous/projective/receptive
P84 animals/

Printed in the United Kingdom
by Lightning Source UK Ltd.
130429UK00001BA/8/A